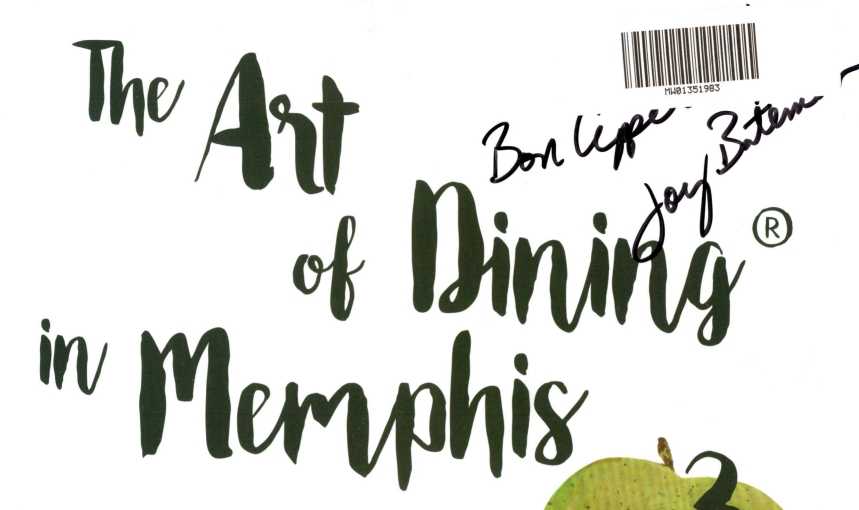

The Art of Dining in Memphis®

A Restaurant Guide with Signature Recipes

Joy Bateman

author illustrator publisher

To my dear friends with whom I have shared many a meal for well over a fourth of a century. Amy, Gigi, Jean, Jeanie, and Leslie.

The Art of Dining® in Memphis 3

Library of Congress Cataloging-in-Publishing-Data
ISBN 978-0-9773226-7-1
Printed in the United States of America

Copyright © 2016 · Joy Gingold Bateman

All rights reserved. No part of this book may be reproduced or transmitted in any form or by any means, electronic or mechanical, including photocopying, recording, or by any information storage and retrieval system, without permission of the publisher.

joysartofdining.com

On the far left is Ben Smith from Tsunami, in the middle is Andrew Adams from Acre; on the right is Erling Jensen. Of course, on the very far right is me, Joy Bateman.

Dear Reader,

My wish for you as well as me, is that we do not go too long without enjoying delicious food. A delectable recipe makes everything better with my world. *"Hey Jude, don't make it bad, take a sad song and make it better."* Yes, I am a Beatles fan—and Rogers & Hammerstein as well.

My love affair with food goes way back, but a decade ago I decided to put pen to paper and *The Art of Dining®* series was born, combining my two loves: painting and good cuisine. I am pleased to present my latest collection of culinary delights, *The Art of Dining® in Memphis 3*. This would not have happened without the 53 local restaurants that were so kind and generous to share their wonderful recipes.

Applause goes to my amazing new editor, Conchita Topinka, who has brought much to the table. New to Memphis by way of Miami, she came to the United States as a small child when her family fled Castro's communist Cuba. Karen Miller from Fernandina Beach, Florida, is my multi-talented recipe editor on her fourth book with me. Less than two years ago she published her own book, *Succotash Dreams*. Pamela McFarland, my genius graphic designer, is also on her fourth book with me.

The Art of Dining® in Memphis 3 is for all foodies. Those with discerning palates and those with, well, not so much. Everyone is welcome through the many doors I have painted for this book. I invite you to step into this wonderland of local cuisine.

Enjoy winning recipes from a variety of Memphis eateries—Italian, Mexican, Mediterranean, Ethiopian, Thai, Chinese, French, American and Japanese. There are also bars where cuisine rules, and of course, Bar-B-Q—just a few.

And look for my dozen dishes, which, I do declare, are delicious and dazzling enough to share.

Truffles and caviar, by chance? They will make your taste buds dance! No crumpets and tea. It's chicken livers for me! Take a look. . . it's in this book.

For a crowd, or just a few, let's eat, drink, and skip to my Lou!

Bon Appetit,

Joy Bateman

When you rise in the morning , give thanks for the light, for your Life , for your Strength. Give thanks for your food and for the joy of Living.–Tecumseh (1768–1813)

Acre	6
Andrew Michael Italian Kitchen	8
Beauty Shop	10
Belle - A Southern Bistro	12
Bhan Thai	14
Blue Nile Ethiopian	16
Booksellers Bistro	18
Bounty on Broad	20
Brother Juniper's	22
Café 1912	24
Café Eclectic	26
Café Palladio	28
Calvary Waffle Shop	30
Casablanca	32
Chez Philippe	34
Ciao Bella	36
Ecco	38
Erling Jensen	40
The Farmer	42
Felicia Suzanne's	44
Fino's East	46
Flight Restaurant & Wine Bar	48
Folk's Folly Original Prime Steak House	50
The Grove Grill	52
Hog & Hominy	54
Interim	56
Itta Bena	58
Jim's Place	60
The Kitchen	62
Las Tortugas	64

Table of Contents

The Little Tea Shop - - - - - - - - - - - - - - - - - 66
McEwen's on Monroe - - - - - - - - - - - - - - - 68
Mesquite Chop House - - - - - - - - - - - - - - - 70
Napa Café - 72
Panda Garden - 74
Paulette's - 76
Porcellino's Craft Butcher - - - - - - - - - - - - - 78
Restaurant Iris - 80
The Second Line - - - - - - - - - - - - - - - - - - - 82
South Main Sushi & Grill - - - - - - - - - - - - - 84
Staks - 86
Strano! Sicilian Kitchen & Bar - - - - - - - - 88
Sweet Grass - 90
Tsunami - 92
Woman's Exchange - - - - - - - - - - - - - - - - 94
Two From the Past - - - - - - - - - - - - - - - - - 96
Seven From Heaven - - - - - - - - - - - - - - - - 97

Delta Blues Winery - - - - - - - - - - - - - - - - 98
Bardog Tavern - - - - - - - - - - - - - - - - - - - 100
The Cove - 101
The 5 Spot - 102
Huey's - 103
Bar-B-Q Shop - - - - - - - - - - - - - - - - - - - 104
Central BBQ - 105
Elwood's Shack - - - - - - - - - - - - - - - - - - 106
Payne's Bar-B-Q - - - - - - - - - - - - - - - - - 107
A Dozen Dishes - - - - - - - - - - - - - - - - - - 108
About Joy Bateman - - - - - - - - - - - - - - - 112

Acre Restaurant

690 South Perkins   901.818.2273

High Expectations

After returning home from vacation at a lovely 6,000 acre ranch in Snow Mass, Colorado, I stepped into Acre and for a minute thought maybe I had never left Snow Mass. High vaulted ceilings of rustic wood, solid wood tables, contemporary benches, chairs and couches, and beautiful large sepia photographs of horses set the mood in this classy, upscale restaurant. Lunch at Acre is a treat. The Seared Maine Sea Scallops with baby carrots, squash, Sea Island peas, and tomato vinaigrette is exquisite. Dinner at Acre is sublime. Fried Soft Shell Crab when in season is not to miss. For the daring and brave there's Grilled Spanish Octopus with gigante beans, black garlic, oxtail, and gochujang. Talented and passionate, chefs Wally Joe and Andrew Adams are the masterminds of this innovative seasonal American cuisine. Having the two in one place doubles the pleasure.

Pork Ragu

Ingredients:

2 oz butter
1½ oz minced onions
3 oz minced carrots
1½ minced celery
3 oz quartered mushrooms
1¾ pounds 1 inch diced pork butt
16 oz. milk
16 oz. red wine
3 pounds canned diced tomatoes

Preparation:

Heat oven to 400 degrees. Melt butter in a large pot. Add onions, carrots, celery, and mushrooms, and sweat for about 2 minutes. In the oven on a sheet pan or cookie sheet, heat pork butt for 10 minutes. Drain the fat from the pork, and add it to the vegetables in the pot. Add the milk, and cook on medium heat until it has reduced to almost dry. Add the wine, and cook on medium heat until it has reduced to almost dry. Add the tomatoes, and cook on low for about 3 more hours. Crush the pork pieces to break up. Serve over pasta, rice, vegetables, or just by itself with a piece of cornbread.

White Chocolate Cherry Scones

Ingredients:

2¾ pounds bread flour
10½ oz. granulated sugar
2½ oz. baking powder
1 oz. salt
2 oz. dried cherries (rehydrated for 30 minutes in hot water)
12 oz. white chocolate chips
1 pound heavy whipping cream
butter or cooking spray as needed for coating the pan
flour as needed for rolling the dough out
milk & sugar as needed for topping

Preparation:

Preheat oven to 360 degrees. Grease a cookie sheet with butter or pan spray. In a mixer with a paddle attachment, mix flour, sugar, baking powder, and salt until well blended. This recipe can be mixed by hand or a spoon. Add the drained cherries and chocolate chips. Add the cream, and mix just until blended. Turn the mixture onto a heavily floured table. Roll the dough to about 1 inch thickness. Cut the scones into 2½ inch triangles or whatever shape works best for you. Put the scones onto the greased baking sheet about ½ inch apart, and brush with a little milk. Sprinkle a little sugar on top. Either cook the scones at this point or freeze them for another time.

Bake the scones in the oven for about 20 minutes until golden brown and cooked all the way through. Cooking time may vary greatly due to the size of the scones and different ovens and cooking trays.

Andrew Michael Italian Kitchen

712 West Brookhaven Circle   901.347.3569

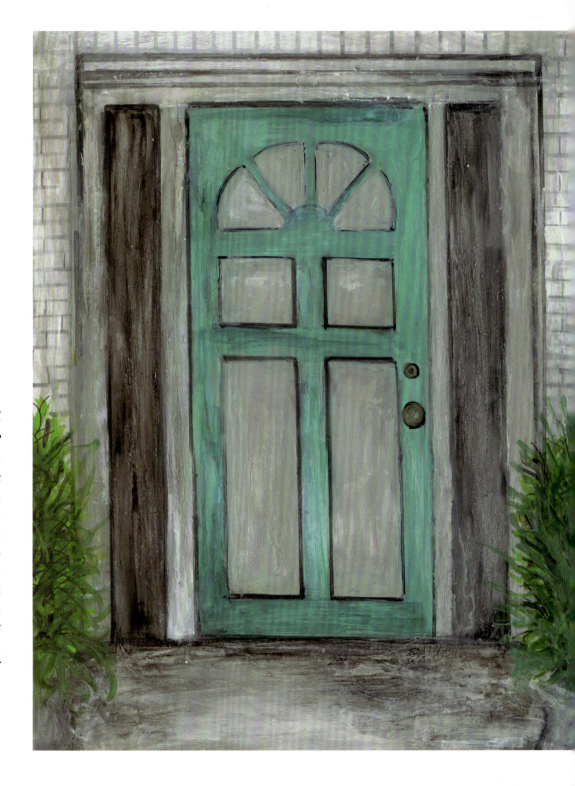

Blissfully Satisfying

A foodie's paradise? Sophisticated menu? Creative and interesting? Blissfully satisfied when you leave? YES to all the above. Since 2009, owner-chefs Andrew Ticer and Michael Hudman continue to make hay while the sun shines (and great pasta, too!) To guide you through the gathering. . . Lonzo di Toscana, Chicken Liver Parfait, Peperone. To begin. . . Sweetbreads, Scallops. To nourish. . . Maw Maw's Ravioli, Potato Gnocchi. And of course the Casonsei, featured in Memphis *magazine's City Guide as one of the Top Ten Dishes of 2016. To continue. . . Newman Farm Pork, Halibut, Duck, Ocean Trout. Michael Hudman and Andrew Ticer have won multiple James Beard awards, and in 2015, Andrew Michael Italian Kitchen was named in the international ultimate insiders' guide,* Where Chefs Eat, *recommended by Chris Shepherd. "They're smart cooks. They do well-presented food," said Shepherd. Closer to home,* Memphis—*listed them in the Who's Who of Memphis.*

Saffron Risotto

Ingredients:

6–8 cups chicken stock
½ bunch fresh flat-leaf parsley
½ bunch fresh thyme
Large pinch saffron threads
¼ cup unsalted butter
2 Tablespoons olive oil
1 large yellow onion, finely diced
2 stalks celery, finely diced
½ pound chicken gizzards, cleaned and finely chopped
1½ cups Arborio rice
½ cup dry white wine
4 oz. Parmigiano Reggiano cheese, grated

Preparation:

In a saucepan, bring the stock to a light simmer and add the parsley, thyme, and saffron. Reduce the heat to very low and keep warm. Warm a saucepan over medium heat, and add the butter and oil. When the butter melts, add the onion and sauté until translucent, about 10 minutes. Add celery, and sauté until softened, about 5 minutes. Add gizzards, and sauté until cooked through, about 15 minutes. Add the rice, and stir until it starts to give off a nutty aroma, about 30 seconds. Stir in wine, and cook until slightly reduced. Ladle about 1 cup of stock into the pan, and cook, stirring constantly with a wooden spoon, until the liquid is absorbed. Continue to cook, adding the stock about 1 cup at a time, until the rice is tender but the center of each grain is still slightly firm, 15–20 minutes. Remove risotto from the heat and stir in half of the cheese. Divide the risotto among warmed, wide, shallow bowls, and garnish with the remaining cheese. Serve immediately. Serves 4.

Beauty Shop

966 South Cooper   901.272.7111

Pamper Your Taste Buds

Sunday brunch at the Beauty Shop is eye-popping. Whether it is the Chicken & Waffle, Steak & Egg, Chileques Migas, Eggs Florentine with fried Gulf oysters, or the "Egg in da hole" One-Eyed Jack, it's all extremely satisfying. You'll feel pampered—even if you don't get to sit under one of the old-school hooded dryers. Fun, funky, and artsy. At night, the Beauty Shop takes a turn into a serene, relaxed atmosphere. The lights dim, romance sets in, and the cuisine continues to win. The ever-changing menu ensures the very freshest ingredients of the season. Let's hope for cast iron Lamb Loin Chops, pan-roasted Barramundi, Crispy Duck, maple-glazed Benton's bacon-wrapped Filet Mignon with Frites, Thai Steak Salad, or Romenesca Cauliflower. Award-winning owner/chef Karen Carrier remains on fire. Her creativity and energy never seem to tire.

Jamaican Meat Patties

Pastry Ingredients:

2 cups all purpose flour
¼ teaspoon salt
¼ teaspoon lard
½ stick margarine
⅓ cup of cold water

Preparation:

In a medium bowl sift the flour and salt till well combined. Cut in the lard and margarine till flour starts to crumble, and add the cold water to make a stiff dough. Lightly flour work surface, and roll out the dough to ⅛ inch thick. Cut out rounds with a small biscuit cutter.

Filling Ingredients:

2 Tablespoons unsalted butter
1 small white onion, finely chopped
¼ teaspoon chopped scotch bonnet pepper
½ pound ground chuck
½ teaspoon salt
½ teaspoon black pepper
½ teaspoon curry powder
½ teaspoon ground allspice
½ teaspoon dried thyme
¼ cup bread crumbs
¼ cup chicken stock
1 egg, beaten
¼ cup water

Preparation:

Preheat oven to 400 degrees. Place a small skillet over medium high heat for one minute. Add the butter, and sauté the onion and scotch bonnet peppers together till onions are slightly translucent. Add the beef, salt, pepper, curry, allspice, and thyme, and mix well. Brown the meat for 10 minutes, stirring occasionally. Once the meat has browned, add the bread crumbs and stock, and combine well. Cover the skillet, and simmer for 15 minutes, stirring occasionally. When all liquids have been absorbed, the filling is ready. Taste for seasoning. It should be moist but not watery.

Set mixture aside, and begin making your patties. On a clean surface, roll out the dough to ⅛-inch thick. Using a 3-inch biscuit cutter, cut the dough into rounds. Moisten the edges of the dough with an egg wash, and place a small amount of the beef mixture in the center of the patty. Fold the dough over the filling to form a half-moon shape, and pinch the edges closed with a fork. Lightly brush the top of the pastry with more egg wash. Place patties on a greased baking sheet, and bake in oven till pastry is lightly golden. Serve with Pick-A-Peppa sauce for dipping.

Belle: A Southern Bistro

117 Union Avenue   901.433.9851

Tasty Southern Hospitality

A building that was built in 1905 has a striking new modern marbled front with a red awning. Oh my! Beyond the glass door is the chic charcuterie and wine bar. Next is a long, handsome bar of dark, polished wood—all hand-made from shoe racks—which matches the paneling behind the church pews with emerald green seats. Ever so charming! Wait, there's more. Try the Bonnie Blue Goat Cheese Balls, Sweet Potato Chipotle, or the exquisite Lobster Ravioli with Black truffle butter and Arkansas Caviar. Entrees range from Blackened Salmon to Sliced Glazed Brisket—Bourbon brown-sugar glazed with roasted garlic mashed potatoes and fried tobacco onions. I admit unashamedly this brisket was the most flavorful I have ever had. Maybe one exception, my cousin Cathy's in B'ham, Ala. Kudos to Chef David Johnson.

Warm Crab Baked Avocado

Ingredients:

2 avocados, not too firm to the touch, cut in half and seeded
2 limes, juiced
4 oz. lump crabmeat, picked free of any shells
½ stick unsalted butter, cut into Tablespoon-size pieces
Salt
Pepper
Olive Oil

Preparation:

Preheat oven to 400 degrees. Place avocados, skin side down in a sauté pan. Drizzle flesh with olive oil, and sprinkle with salt and pepper. Bake in oven 15 minutes or until soft to touch.

While avocado is baking, place ½ tablespoon of butter and crabmeat in a small sauté pan over low heat just to warm up. In a small saucepan, bring lime juice to boil over medium heat. As soon as lime juice starts to boil, whisk in 1 Tablespoon butter until completely melted. Turn heat to low, and add butter 1 Tablespoon at a time until melted. Remove from heat, and add salt to taste. Place warm crabmeat in seed cavity of the baked avocados, and ladle lime butter over crab. Garnish with sliced green onions or chopped parsley if desired. Serves 2.

Bhan Thai

1324 Peabody   901.272.1538

Consistent Authenticity

Escape for a little Thai, and leave your passport at home. Bodacious flavors await you at Bhan Thai. Experience authenticity not only in the food but in the atmosphere and décor. Add a spacious patio, and there you have it: perfect harmony. Order from an extensive menu of innovative and dazzling dishes perfectly prepared by Chef Sorrasit "Alex" Sittranont. House specialties include Salmon Panang, Crispy Duck, Northern Thai Curry Chicken, and Garlic Pork Chops. As an appetizer for two, the Thai Toast was my pick. Totally unique with a little kick. Owner Molly Smith is an exceptional restaurateur and has the votes coming in year after year. From 2003, the year after she opened, to the present, Bhan Thai has been voted "Best Thai" in Memphis magazine's Readers' Restaurant Poll.

Bhan Thai Toast

Ingredients:

10 oz. raw shrimp, peeled and deveined
2 teaspoons soy sauce
1 egg
4–5 garlic cloves, chopped
7–8 cilantro roots, roughly chopped
¼ teaspoon white pepper
½ teaspoon salt
Choice of white bread cut in triangles or sliced French bread
3 Tablespoons sesame seeds
Peanut oil or vegetable oil

Preparation:

Using a food processor or blender, whiz the shrimp into a smooth paste. Transfer to a bowl, add the soy sauce and egg, and mix well. Let set approximately 30 minutes. Pound the garlic, cilantro roots, white pepper, and salt into a smooth paste. Add to the shrimp paste. Spread the shrimp paste on one side of each bread piece, then sprinkle with sesame seeds. Refrigerate for 30 minutes. Heat oil in a deep frying pan over medium heat. Test oil to make sure it sizzles and you know the oil is ready. Deep fry a few slices of toast at a time, paste side down, for 3 minutes or until golden. Turn with a slotted spoon. Drain paste side up on a paper towel. Serve with cucumber salad.

Blue Nile Ethiopian Kitchen

1788 Madison   901.474.7214

More Kabobs Please

Kabobs? Did someone say kabobs? Blue Nile has it going on. Classic Ethiopian authentic cuisine is mouth-watering at Blue Nile Ethiopian Kitchen on Madison Avenue. It all began with their sister food truck Stickem. Yay for Stickem! Yay for kabobs! The menu features tasty offerings such as Doro Wat (rich and savory chicken) and Yeager Wat (delicious and bold lamb stew). The beet salad with onion and jalapeños is light, delish, and always on my radar. Check out the beautiful, expansive mural by Gina Sposto. The large bright and colorful lions are watching! Now, let's get to the dessert… the Tiramisu is ambrosial.

Lamb Burger

Ingredients:

2 pounds ground lamb
2–4 oz. fresh garlic
5–7 sticks fresh rosemary
1 cup olive oil
¼ cup fresh lemon juice
3 jalapeños with seeds removed
Salt and pepper
Lettuce
Tomato
Onion
Bread or buns

Preparation:
For patties, puree 2 oz. of garlic and rosemary in blender or food processor with a dash of water or oil, and then mix with the ground lamb, salt, and pepper to taste. Portion into six 8-oz. patties, and set aside.

For Dressing:

Blend olive oil, lemon juice, remaining garlic, and rosemary, jalapeños with salt and pepper to taste.

Cook patties on grill or in pan. In a bowl, combine lettuce, tomato, and onion, and toss with dressing. Toast bread/buns and place a patty on each bun. Put lettuce mix on top, and drizzle top piece of bun with remaining dressing

The Booksellers Bistro

387 Perkins Extended   901.374.0881

Brain Food

"In the early mornin' rain, with a dollar in my hand. . ." Canadian singer-songwriter Gordon Lightfoot gets my attention as well as breakfast at Booksellers Bistro. Must be the atmosphere. Opening early at 7:30, I love that it is quiet and relaxing. Even nostalgic. As the day continues, added energy and zeal make it real. Any meal, any time of day, is most conducive for conversation here whether it be with family and friends, or a business meeting. Jennifer Chandler's Tuscan Chicken Sandwich, the Skip Jack Tuna Melt, and Spinach Artichoke Quesadillas are all excellent choices for lunch. Year-round, after five, the Shrimp and Polenta wins the prize. The Chicken Piccata, I could eat a lotta, though it is offered winter only. The sensational signature soup of Tomato Blue Cheese is splendid indeed. Now let's go read. Booksellers Bistro is in a bookstore!

Tomato Bleu Cheese Soup

Ingredients:

¼ oz. butter
1 yellow onion
1 Tablespoon minced garlic
1 cup flour
1½ quarts water
Two 32-oz. cans diced tomatoes
½ pound bleu cheese
1–2 Tablespoons salt
1 teaspoon white pepper
1 cup heavy cream

Preparation:

Melt butter, dice onions, and sauté until translucent, along with the garlic. Add flour to make a roux. (Be careful not to burn.) Whisk water into roux until smooth. Add diced tomatoes, bleu cheese, salt, and pepper. Bring to a boil, and turn off heat. Add cream. Puree with hand blender or food processor. Serves 6–8.

Bounty on Broad

2519 Broad   910.410.8131

Broad Appeal

boun-ty/n/· good things that are given in large amounts

There is definitely plenty to like at Bounty on Broad. When you visit this popular addition to Broad Street's eclectic vibe, you better bring a big appetite or be willing to share. A seasonal menu using the freshest ingredients available features exceedingly large portions served family style. The Slow Cooked Beets and Pommes Frites are delightful. And you can't go wrong with the Braised Pork Shank with Smoked Gouda Grits and Greens. Dessert is a must have, with several to choose from. My choice was the Banana Bread Split with vanilla ice cream, chocolate ganache, toasted almonds, and, why not? a cherry on top! It was awesome, no less. The talented Pastry Chef Natasha Casey is the wife of Chef Russell Casey.

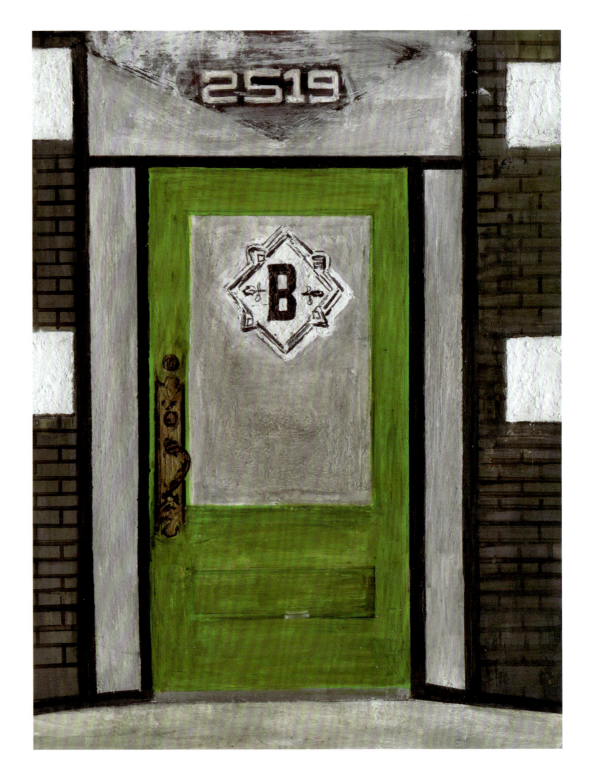

White Wine and Fresh Herb Braised Pork Cheeks

Ingredients:

5 pounds pork cheeks
1 medium yellow onion, diced
3 large carrots, diced
2 whole stalks celery, diced
1 whole fennel bulb, top removed, diced
4 heirloom tomatoes, diced
10 cloves fresh garlic, crushed
1 cup fresh thyme leaves, stems removed and minced
6 sprigs fresh rosemary
2 cups white cooking wine
Chicken or pork stock
Kosher salt and black pepper to taste

Preparation:

Clean pork cheeks by removing any excess skin and sinew, thus exposing the meaty part of the pork cheeks. Season both sides with salt, black pepper, olive oil, and half the chopped fresh thyme. Allow cheeks to sit covered at room temperature for 2 hours. Add oil to a Rondeau-sized pot on medium heat, and place on the stovetop. Lightly dust the pork cheeks in rice flour. Add to pot, and sear about 4 minutes per side or until golden brown. Remove cheeks from pot.

Add more olive oil to the pot, and bring back to temperature on medium high heat. Add tomatoes, remaining chopped thyme, rosemary sprigs, and white wine. Bring to a simmer, and scrape the bottom of the pan. You are essentially deglazing the pan. Reduce the liquid by one third. Add cheeks back to the pot. Add enough stock until the cheeks are completely covered. Place a lid on the pot or cover with foil. Place in a 300 degree oven for 2–3 hours or until fork tender.

Brother Juniper's

3519 Walker   901.324.0144

A Faithful Following

It's no wonder that year after year, the family-run Brother Juniper's wins "Best Breakfast" in Memphis magazine Readers' Restaurant Poll. Witty Patrick, organized and efficient Sarah, angelic Pauline, and passionate Jonathan keep Brother Juniper's alive and well. What to order? The Special Gyro on a Warm Pita is a great place to start. My youngest son, William, swears by the Chorizo Sausage Burrito. Brother Juniper's sumptuous original and creative omelets certainly make it worth getting out of bed in the morning. And don't forget the open-face omelet options! Spinach is featured in numerous dishes at Brother Juniper's—don't tell anyone, but I've heard Popeye may be a distant relative. The Koplin family makes "Food, Family, and Community" its key ingredients. This "Best Breakfast in the Nation" winner hosts a monthly Community Spotlight to raise money for local charitable organizations that help those in need.

Garden and Lamb Omelet

Ingredients:

Vegetable oil
Butter
4 slices gyro meat (lamb)
1 cup fresh spinach
¼ cup chopped tomatoes
2 Tablespoons chopped green onions
3 eggs, beaten
¼ cup mozzarella cheese
¼ cup crumbled feta cheese

Preparation:

In skillet, sauté gyro meat in vegetable oil for two minutes over medium heat. Add spinach, tomatoes, and green onion, sauté until cooked through, and set aside. Melt butter in another skillet and add beaten eggs on low to medium heat. As eggs cook, keep folding under until most of the egg is absorbed. Then flip over and cook for another 30 seconds. Cover omelet with vegetable and meat mixture, top with cheese, and serve.

Café 1912

243 South Cooper   901.722.2700

Cooper's French Connection

The Onion Soup Gratinee rules at Café 1912. It sets the standard for all the other fine offerings at this cozy French-inspired bistro. Or you can start your French escape with the memorable Pommes Frites with Parmesan Cheese. Glenn Hays, a well-known and respected restaurateur, knows his business. This neighborhood jewel of a café was opened by Hays and his wife Martha in September 2002. Located in an early twentieth-century building, it's a favorite among locals and something I'm sure more tourists wish they knew about. I have always been a fan of the Veal Piccata—a prize-winning entrée for sure! Wait, there's more... Coq au Vin, Goat Cheese-Stuffed Scallops, Maple-Glazed Salmon, and Lyonnaise and Nicoise salads. The very good Burgers are served with Pommes Frites, of course. If you leave room for dessert, you'll have a strikingly tasty selection from which to choose.

Amaretto Goat Cheese Cheesecake

Ingredients:

One 9-inch springform pan with graham cracker crust on the bottom only
6 oz. goat cheese, softened
1 pound cream cheese, softened
¾ cup sour cream
1 whole egg
½ Tablespoon vanilla
1 Tablespoon amaretto (can be increased for a stronger taste)
1 cup sugar

Preparation:

Mix cheese in mixer with the paddle attachment until smooth. Add sour cream, and continue to mix. Add egg, making sure it incorporates. Fold in remaining ingredients, and mix well. Pour into springform pan, and bake at 325 degrees for 45 minutes to an hour. (Use the knife test to check if it is done.) Cool overnight. (The cheesecake must cool and set before it can be served.)

Ingredients for Graham Cracker Crust:

1½ cups finely ground graham cracker crumbs
⅓ cup white sugar
6 tablespoons of melted butter
Vanilla to taste

Preparation:

Mix together, and push into the bottom of a 9-inch springform pan.

Café Eclectic

603 North McLean   901.725.1718

Come On In!

Warm and inviting, this happy neighborhood cafe welcomes all. I have said it before, and I will say it again: I love Rachel's Breakfast Wrap at Cafe Eclectic. It is always a home run. The French Omelet is a close second. A three-egg omelet stuffed with fresh spinach and white cheddar, topped with sour cream. Top-notch! On the lighter side. . . house-made yogurt and honey topped with fresh berries is tasty and healthy to boot. On weekends, get creative with choices such as Dr. Love's Bird and Biscuit and the Bird Benedict. Lunch offers seductive sandwiches and wraps, burgers, dogs, and mom's home recipe of Chicken Pot Pie. The Strawberry Fields Salad, since day one, sassy as ever. It's not over yet. There's a House Bakery and Soda Fountain, substantial as a mountain. Time for one more Illy cup.

Carrot Cake

Ingredients:

2 cups sugar
1 cup softened butter
4 eggs
4 cups all-purpose flour
2 teaspoons baking powder
2 teaspoons ground cinnamon
1½ teaspoons baking soda
1 teaspoon salt
18-oz. can crushed pineapple (drain well)
2 cups grated carrots
1½ cups flaked coconut

For the frosting:

16 oz. cream cheese, softened
1 cup butter, softened
2 teaspoons vanilla extract
5 cups confectioners' sugar

Preparation:

In a large bowl, cream the butter and sugar together. Add eggs one at a time, beating well after each addition. Blend together well. In another large bowl, combine the flour, baking powder, cinnamon, baking soda, and salt; gradually beat in sugar mixture until blended. Stir in the pineapple, carrots, and coconut. The batter will be thick. Transfer to three greased and floured 9-inch round baking pans. Bake at 350 degrees for 35–40 minutes. Let cake cool for 10 minutes.

For the frosting, in a large bowl, beat the cream cheese, butter, and vanilla until fluffy. Gradually add confectioners' sugar. Frost each layer, and spread remaining frosting over the top and sides of the cake, covering the entire cake evenly. Cover and store in the refrigerator.

A party without cake is just a meeting – Julia Child

Café Palladio

2169 Central   901.278.0129

Browse and Dine

Enjoy a touch of casual elegance at this charming café in one of Memphis' finest antique galleries. Gorgeous, rustic chandeliers above, surrounded by art, china, lamps, tables and chairs, antique and contemporary. For sandwiches Café Palladio offers River-City Panini, Rueben-Esque, Ham and Pear, Chunky Chicken Salad (their signature sandwich), and the Garden Dagwood. Soups change daily but if it happens to be mushroom, GO FOR IT! So fabulous. Entrée Salads include Greek, Spinach and Fruit, BLT Salad, Cranapple and Cobb. For dessert: the memorable Coconut Cake, listed among our Best Sweets on page 97. Also offered are the very popular Strawberry and Caramel cakes from Sugaree's Bakery.

Carolina Pimento Cheese

Ingredients:

2 cups extra sharp cheddar cheese, shredded
½ cup cream cheese, softened
½ cup real mayonnaise
¼ teaspoon each onion powder, granulated garlic, and ground cayenne
4-oz. jar pimentos, drained
Salt and pepper to taste

Preparation:

Combine all ingredients (other than pimentos) in food processor or in large bowl of mixer. Blend at medium speed until thoroughly combined. Add pimentos, and continue blending for a additional 15–20 seconds.

Mushroom Soup

Ingredients:

1 stick butter
2 garlic cloves, minced
¼ cup diced yellow onions
¼ cup diced carrots
¼ cup diced celery
1 pound sliced mushrooms
2 Tablespoons flour
2 cups chicken or vegetable stock
1 cup half-and-half
Salt and pepper
Dried thyme
Nutmeg
Parsley or rosemary sprigs

Preparation:

Melt butter in stock pot, and add garlic, mushrooms, onion, carrots, and celery. Cook until tender, and add a dash of thyme until fragrant, about 1 minute. Whisk in flour until flour browns.

Add chicken/vegetable stock, and cook until slightly thickened (can add cooked diced chicken for a variation). Stir in half-and-half until heated throughout. Season with salt, pepper, and nutmeg according to taste. Garnish with parsley or rosemary sprigs, if desired.

Calvary Waffle Shop

102 North Second Street   901.525.6602

Food For The Soul

The volunteer-run Waffle Shop at Calvary Episcopal Church has been a Memphis tradition since 1928. I'm proud to say that in 1983, I was one of those volunteers with two toddlers in tow. So much fun! The Waffle Shop is a gathering place for folk of all faiths—Episcopalians, other faiths, and perhaps no faith at all, who enjoy great food. Each year during Lent, a scrumptious lunch is served with proceeds going to support the outreach ministries of congregations throughout Memphis. Still serving some of the original recipes from 1928, the Waffle Shop serves up good food for a good cause… Seafood Gumbo, Shrimp Mousse, Corned Beef with Cabbage, Waffles & Chicken Hash, Waffles and Sausage, Chicken Salad and Tomato Aspic, Boston Cream Pie, Schaum Torte, Chocolate Bourbon Cake, and Peppermint Ice Cream with Chocolate Sauce. Must I say more? Will not disappoint!

Fish Pudding

Ingredients:

2½ pounds cod or catfish fillets
2½ Tablespoons grated onion
¼ cup lemon juice
¼ cup melted butter
¼ cup cracker crumbs
1½ teaspoons salt
2 cups milk
1 small dash Tabasco Sauce
½ cup chopped parsley
6 eggs, beaten
2 Tablespoons dry sherry

Preparation:

Grease a large casserole dish with butter, and set aside. Mix all the ingredients together well, and pour into prepared pan. Cover with cracker crumbs, and dot generously with butter. Bake at 375 degrees for 30–40 minutes or until firm and golden brown on top.

Calvary Waffle Shop Mayonnaise

Ingredients:

5 egg yolks
½ gallon vegetable oil
½ cup lemon juice
1 Tablespoon Dijon mustard
1 Tablespoon Worcestershire Sauce
1½ teaspoons Tabasco Sauce
1½ teaspoons salt
  A little paprika for just the right color

Preparation:

Beat egg yolks until whipped. Slowly add ½ gallon oil and lemon juice. Add mustard, Worcestershire Sauce, Tabasco Sauce, and salt on high speed until all is incorporated.

Casablanca Restaurant

1707 Madison   901.421.6949

Exotic and Delectable

Casablanca's décor captures the Mediterranean/Moroccan mystique of its memorable cuisine. Nestled behind tall trees on Madison Avenue, a lovely outdoor patio awaits you. Walk up the steps of lattice wood, and you'll find wrought iron chairs and tables dressed with white tablecloths and blue linen napkins to match the front door. The interior has a generous selection of Mediterranean and Moroccan vases, curtains, and chandeliers. The Jerusalem Salad is sensational. I love that they peel the cucumber. Most places do not. Other popular dishes: Kibbeh, Baba Ghanoush, Shawerma, Moussaka, Egyptian Hawawshi and Kabobs. The Sri Lankan tea is excellent—hot or cold. It's made with a savory combination of honey, sage, and ginger. The East Memphis location on Poplar features the same great food.

Moroccan Soup

Ingredients:

½ red onion, finely chopped
Four stalks celery, chopped
¼ cup extra virgin olive oil
Four tomatoes, diced
12 oz. tomato paste
1 package chick peas, soaked overnight in water,
    or 1 can cooked chick peas
½ package lentils
¼ cup parsley, chopped
¼ cup cilantro, chopped
½ teaspoon paprika
Salt and pepper

Preparation:

Cook onions and celery in olive oil until soft. Add diced tomatoes, and continue to cook a few minutes longer. Remove from stove. Add the mixture to a large pot with 2 quarts of water and tomato paste. Add chick peas and lentils. Add parsley, cilantro, and spices. Bring to a boil, and then simmer for 20–30 minutes, stirring occasionally, until chick peas and lentils are tender. Season with salt and pepper to taste.

Chez Philippe

149 Union   901.529.4188

Romantic Flair, Exquisite Fare

"Where do I begin
To tell the story of how great a love can be?
The sweet love story that is older than the sea. . ."

I can relate. Chez Philippe comes to me like the song from Love Story. *The ambience, the décor, the classical music, the empyreal service, the out-of-this-world-magnificent presentation of dishes. From the garden, there's Tomato Burrata with house ricotta cream, 25-year-old balsamic, tomato confit, and basil puree. So light and refreshing! Seared Crab Cake with Alabama blue crab, hibiscus barley, and orange beurre blanc is a marvel. Nothing like it. Located at the East side of the grand lobby of the Peabody Hotel, Chez Philippe continues to serve classical/contemporary French cuisine that makes Memphis proud.*

Hemp Seed Crusted Chilean Sea Bass with Braised Red and White Belgian Endive and Lentil Ragout

Ingredients:

28 oz. Chilean sea bass, cut in 4 portions
1 oz. shelled hempseed
1 egg yolk

Ingredients for Lentil Ragout

2 oz. black lentils
1 zucchini, cut in ¼ inch cube
1 yellow squash, cut in ¼ inch cube
2 Roma tomatoes, cut in ¼ inch cube
1 bunch green onion, cut small
1 grilled portabella mushroom, cut in ¼ inch cube
1 onion
2 cloves
2 garlic cloves
1 bay leaf
1 sprig rosemary
1 sprig fresh thyme
2 slices applewood bacon (optional)
⅛ cup heavy cream
1 Tablespoon butter

Ingredients for Braised Belgian Endive

2 white Belgian endive
2 red Belgian endive

¼ cup port wine
¼ cup orange juice
1 pinch sugar in the raw
1 oz. butter

Ingredients for Sauce

½ cup white wine
¼ cup fish stock
⅛ cup heavy cream
6 oz. butter
1 whole lemon

Preparation:

Coat sea bass with hemp seed, then set aside in refrigerator. In water, cook black lentils, and add in a sachet of the rosemary, thyme, 2 cloves, bay leaf, garlic, onions, and cook with lentils until the lentils are tender but not overcooked, and then strain the liquid and set aside. While the lentils are cooking, cut zucchini, yellow squash, tomatoes, green onion, grill the mushrooms, and blanch the zucchini and yellow squash in boiling water, drain and shock in ice water. When lentils are cooked, discard the sachet and add vegetables. Mix all ingredients, heat, and set aside.

Braise red endive in port wine, and braise white endive in orange juice. Set aside, and keep warm.

Preparation for sauce:

Place white wine fish stock in small sauce pan, reduce, add cream and reduce to half, then wisk the butter slowly into sauce. Add lemon juice and finish with salt and pepper. Keep warm and set aside. In a skillet, carefully sear sea bass, coated side first; then turn on other side, and place in 375 degree oven. Cook for 6–8 minutes. For presentation leave room for your imagination.

Ciao Bella Italian Grill

565 Erin Drive   901.202.2500

Benvenuto!

Ciao Bella is nestled away in a shopping center on Erin Drive, but you won't want to miss this family-owned gem with a tasty blend of Italian and Greek cuisine. I was pleasantly surprised, more like blown away, with their sensational soups. The Avgolemono, Greek soup with lemon, chicken, and orzo, and the Pureed White Bean with Pancetta and Rosemary are amazing. The menu offers an ample selection of pasta dishes, but the Scallops Alla Hammond, served with Chef's Choice of Risotto, is definitely something to consider. Love it! I would be remiss if I did not mention Ciao Bella's Beer Battered Eggplant Fries. A memorable way to begin your visit.

Capellini Toscana

Ingredients:

8 oz. dry capellini/angel hair pasta
4 oz. julienned roasted red bell peppers
2 oz. capers
6 oz. cubed Roma tomatoes
4 oz. quartered artichoke hearts
4 oz. pitted kalamata olives
1 pinch of dry red chili flakes
1 oz. chiffonade fresh basil
2 cloves minced garlic
3 oz. white dry cooking wine
2 Tablespoons unsalted butter
3 oz. extra virgin olive oil
Salt and pepper to taste

Preparation:

Heat a 12-inch nonstick pan to medium-high heat. Add oil and garlic to pan and sauté for 15 seconds, then add wine and cook for one minute until alcohol cooks out. Add butter and all other ingredients except pasta and basil. In a separate pot, bring 4 cups salted water to a boil, and then add pasta. Cook for 2–4 minutes or until pasta is al dente, drain, and add to cooked vegetables. Toss with fresh basil. Serves 2–3 people.

Ecco

1585 Overton Park 901.410.8200

Excellence Three Times Over

In 2002, Sabina Bachmann made her culinary debut with the hip Fratelli's Market Grill on Main Street. Then she followed up with Fratelli's at Memphis Botanical Garden. My, my is it good and going strong! In summer, hardly a week goes by that I don't indulge in her sensational Avocado Soup. But what is really of note here is Ecco, Sabina's third restaurant. OMG! Sabina has been making magic at Ecco on Overton Park since 2014. Mediterranean-inspired specialties range from rib-eye steaks to seared-scallops to house-made pastas. Not to seem bossy, but you must order the Orange and Fennel Salad with olives and red onion, served with white wine vinaigrette over arugula. Delightful. The orange-glazed Berkshire Pork Chop served with white wine risotto and apple-onion chutney is a killer of a pork chop.

Ecco Peasant Soup

Ingredients:

1 teaspoon oil
1 medium onion, chopped
4 cups shredded Savoy cabbage
Minced garlic
5 cups vegetable broth
2 cans rinsed and partially
  mashed beans
Freshly cracked pepper
Grated Parmesan
Extra virgin olive oil

Preparation:

Heat oil over medium heat in a soup pot. Add 1 medium onion, and cook until softened and lightly browned, 2–3 minutes. Add Savoy cabbage and minced garlic; cook until the cabbage has wilted, 2–3 minutes. Add vegetable broth and beans, and bring to a simmer. Reduce heat to medium-low, partially cover, and simmer until the cabbage is tender, 10–12 minutes. Season with cracked pepper. Sprinkle with freshly grated Parmesan cheese and a drizzle of extra virgin olive oil.

This is a vegetarian version of Peasant Soup. You may add rendered pancetta if you wish.

Ehrling Jensen

1044 South Yates   901.763.3700

A Touch of Sass

Sassy and sophisticated. Erling Jensen's "avant-garde" French, continental cuisine is amazing. The menu changes often. Here's a peek: choose from pristine fish such as Grouper Tempura, Atlantic Halibut, Dover Sole, and Icelandic Cod. For a change of pace, take a look at Pan Fried Buttermilk Quail, Pheasant Stuffed Quail , Buffalo Tenderloin, and a ravishing Rack of Lamb. I would be remiss if I did not mention my all-time favorite. I am smitten with Jumbo Lump Crabmeat with Hollandaise. Beluga caviar can be added. To know Erling is a delight. He innovates and pays attention to detail until everything is just right.I guarantee that here you'll find beauty is everywhere in sight.

Pheasant Sausage Gravy

Ingredients:

2 links pheasant sausage
4 shallots, minced
5 cloves roasted garlic
1 cup demi-glace or
similar brown sauce
2 Tablespoons olive oil
1 cup black coffee
¼ cup cream

Preparation:

Dice sausage, then add with olive oil, shallots, and garlic to a sauté pan. Crisp sausage, and brown shallots and garlic in olive oil for about 5 minutes. Deglaze pan with black coffee, and reduce by one half. Add cream and brown sauce, and bring to a simmer. Serve.

The Farmer

3092 Poplar #11   901.324.2221

At Home On The Farm

Guess who? A Farm-to-Table restaurant. Only the freshest local and regional ingredients. Upscale Southern cuisine. You're right. It's the Farmer! And this Farmer takes comfort food to a mouth-watering new level. For lunch there's Pot Roast, on the menu since day one. It is a slow-cooked Angus brisket, with oven-roasted veggies and natural gravy. So tender, so flavorful. It will knock your socks off! The Mac and Cheese is fabulous. If ordering the the Elegant Salad served at lunch, by all means, get the Creole vinaigrette. For dinner, the innovative, thoughtfully prepared entrée Seared Catfish from Mississippi should be taken quite seriously. To end your meal, the pound cake with fresh fruit and homemade whipped cream is a real treat. A new location has given the Farmer room to spread out and, for the first time, a full bar. The new home in Chickasaw Oaks Mall, has Mac Edwards standing tall.

Sloppy Joes

Ingredients:

3 pounds 80/20 ground beef, local if you can get it
1 yellow onion, ⅜ inch dice
3 celery stalks, ⅜ inch dice
1 carrot, ⅜ inch dice
4 garlic cloves, finely chopped
1 Tablespoon Worcestershire sauce
One 12-oz. can tomato paste
¼ teaspoon ground nutmeg
¼ teaspoon ground cloves
¼ cup cider vinegar
½ cup brown sugar
½ cup catsup
½ teaspoons cayenne
1 teaspoon salt
1 teaspoon black pepper

Preparation:

Brown the ground beef, leaving it chunky. Do not drain. In a separate pot, sauté vegetables. Add ground beef with its juices and all other ingredients. Stir to incorporate, and simmer for 15 minutes. Serve on a high quality bakery bun that's been grilled with butter.

Felicia Suzanne's Restaurant

80 Monroe Suite L-1   901.523.0877

Winning Combinations

Is this what heaven is like? If so, I think I might be ready to go. The Crawfish Hand Pies with horseradish cream took me by surprise. I cannot imagine why. After all, Felicia Willett, who years ago worked under the internationally acclaimed Chef Emeril Lagasse in New Orleans, today just might could teach him a thing or two. Willett's extraordinary talent has earned her numerous honors and awards, but she won the hearts of Memphians with her generous spirit and love for those less fortunate. Felicia Suzanne's is open for lunch on Fridays, when the 25-cent Vodka Martini is extremely popular. But nothing takes a back seat to the award-winning Southern cuisine with Lowcountry, Creole, and Delta influences, using regional fresh seafood, local beef, and locally grown produce.

Pickled Jalapeño Grit Muffins

Ingredients:

1½ cups all purpose flour
1 Tablespoon baking powder
½ teaspoon baking soda
½ teaspoon salt
3 eggs, beaten
¾ cup buttermilk
½ cup melted butter
1 cup cooked grits
1 cup grated cheddar cheese
1 Tablespoon Flo's Pickled Jalapeños, chopped
½ cup caramelized onions
¼ cup chopped parsley
Hot sauce to taste

Preparation:

Preheat oven to 350 degrees. Spray muffin pans. In a large mixing bowl, sift the first 4 ingredients together. In another bowl, mix the egg, buttermilk, butter, and grits. Add the milk mixture to the flour mixture, and mix well. Stir in the cheese, jalapeños, and onions. Season with hot sauce to taste. Spoon batter mixture into the prepared muffin pans. Bake for 35 minutes. Remove from oven, and allow to cool. Serve with Flo's Tomato Jam. Makes 16 muffins.

Fino's East

703 West Brookhaven Circle   901.334.4454

All in the Family

I could be tempted to walk a mile for this incredible, reasonably priced Italian fare. Fino's East is the second location for the family-owned deli in Midtown. There is much to choose from to totally satisfy your palate. Sandwiches, soups, salads, pizzas, pasta. . . they're all consistently tip-top. Open and spacious, this place is perfect for one or your entire office. Or bring Mom and Pop and the whole extended family. The Meatball Sub Sandwich is unforgettable. It's no surprise that desserts at Fino's East are over the top. Tiramisu, Tortes, Cannoli, and luscious cakes. Save room for dessert!

Tomato Onion Salad Dressing

Ingredients:

½ pound white onion, julienned
⅔ pound tomatoes, coarsely chopped
2⅓ cup extra virgin olive oil
⅔ cup vegetable oil
⅔ cup red wine vinegar
2 teaspoons garlic salt
2 teaspoons black pepper
1 Tablespoon dried basil

Preparation:

Combine all ingredients until well blended. Makes approximately 10 servings.

Flight Restaurant & Wine Bar

39 South Main   901.521.8005

Good Things Come In Threes

Well-appointed setting, savvy and stellar service. And choices. Lots of choices. That is Flight. Housed in the beautiful old Brodnax building built in 1916, Flight offers innovative fare that can be paired with a seemingly infinite wine list. Mix and match three entrees and three wine selections in one seating. An array of choices will start your taste buds dancing. . . take a look: Louisiana Redfish, Veal Scallopini, Boursin Stuffed Filet, Scallops Benedict, and Lobster Gnocchi. For a unique appetizer, try the Deviled Eggs and Crispy Gulf Oysters (Delta Moon farm eggs topped with cornmeal dusted oysters and bacon marmalade). Shockingly good! Brunch is also a treat at Flight. Don't forget the Bloody Mary! Owners Tom Powers and Russ Graham recently opened Southern Social, a Germantown locale where Southern culinary creations await in an elegant setting.

Shrimp and Grits

Ingredients:

1 cup white stone-ground grits
2 cups chicken stock
2 cups milk
1 teaspoon each salt and pepper
¾ teaspoon Tabasco Sauce
¾ cup jack cheese
4 Tablespoons unsalted butter
1¼ pound 16/20 shrimp
1 cup white button mushrooms
2 teaspoons minced garlic
1 cup white wine
1 cup lemon juice
½ cup olive oil
½ cup bacon drippings
½ cup applewood smoked bacon
Green onion

Preparation:

In a large stock pot add chicken stock, butter, milk, and Tabasco, and bring to a boil. Slowly whisk in grits, transfer to a double boiler, and cook until they are tender and creamy. Stir in cheese, and season with salt and pepper. Keep warm until shrimp are ready.

Peel and devein shrimp. Cook bacon until it begins to brown, remove from heat, strain, and set aside bacon grease and bacon bits. Heat a large skillet until it's smoking hot, add ½ cup bacon grease. When grease is hot, toss in the shrimp, and cook them half way. Stir in minced garlic and bacon bits, being careful not to burn garlic. Add in mushrooms. Stir in white wine and lemon juice for about 30 seconds or until everything is coated. Add in ½ cup olive oil and green onion. In a dish, place 1 cup white grits. Place 6 shrimp around grits, then top with sauce from the pan.

Flight's Bloody Mary (left) is the most amazing version of that classic cocktail that I've ever encountered.

But what to do for cozy brunches at home?

On a Saturday morning not long ago, I discovered Papi Joe from Rossville, Tennessee at the Memphis Farmer's Market. He is known for his Tennessee Pepper Sauce and makes a mean Bloody Mary! His personal recipe, called Papi's Sassy Bloody Mary Mix, is available for purchase at the Farmer's Market, or at joe@papijoes.com.

Folk's Folly Original Prime Steak House

551 South Mendenhall   901.762.8200

Award-winning Tradition

Locally owned Folk's Folly is much more than a steakhouse. Since 1977, the award-winning restaurant has welcomed locals and tourists alike with its jazzy and relaxed yet elegant atmosphere. Begin in the cozy lounge, and try the Famous Fried Dill Pickles. They are divine. On to something more substantial... I'm talking about the USDA prime cuts sourced from Stock Yards in Chicago, a 100-year-old company specializing in Midwestern corn-fed beef. Superbly aged, perfectly cooked, Folk's Folly's jaw-dropping steaks, from 14 oz. to 28 oz., are served sizzling in parsley butter. It's easy to see why this place is revered by loyal clientele. Some of my other favorites include the She-Crab Soup and a Shrimp Cocktail that is out of this world. The Australian Rack of Lamb, range-fed, with rosemary and mint jam, is robust and spectacular—words can not explain!

Bleu Cheese Mountain

Ingredients:

1 cup heavy cream
1 cup half-and-half
2 cups bleu cheese crumbles
Potato chips
¼ cup additional bleu cheese crumbles

Preparation:

Bring half-and-half and heavy cream to simmer in a pan over medium heat, and reduce to about ¾ the amount. Add 2 cups bleu cheese crumbles to pot. Stir until well incorporated and sauce thoroughly coats back of spoon, being careful to not scorch the cream and cheese. Place chips on plate, and ladle cream and cheese mixture over the chips. Sprinkle remaining bleu cheese over the top. Serve warm.

salt & pepper shakers from Ménage Fine Stationery & Gifts

Grove Grill

4550 Poplar   901.818.9951

Flavorful, Fresh Fare

Grove Grill serves up dependable, well-received fare in the high-rent area of Laurelwood in East Memphis. For me and many other Memphians in the sixties this area was our stomping ground, home to Britlings Cafeteria and Brodnax Jewelers. The overwhelming selection of delicious fresh vegetables reflects the insistence on the freshest seasonal ingredients by Owner/Chef Jeff Dunham and crew. The Fig Gorgonzola creation is dynamite. Oyster lovers would be most happy here, with options to choose from including the Cornmeal Fried Oysters with arugula and Creole Remoulade. It's hard to pick a favorite dish, but I can understand why Contemporary Media Publisher Kenneth Neill is taken with the Grove Grill's Roast Chicken with smoked bacon-braised Brussels sprouts and herb pan gravy. Select your favorite, and then accompany it with something from the Grove Grill's generous wine list.

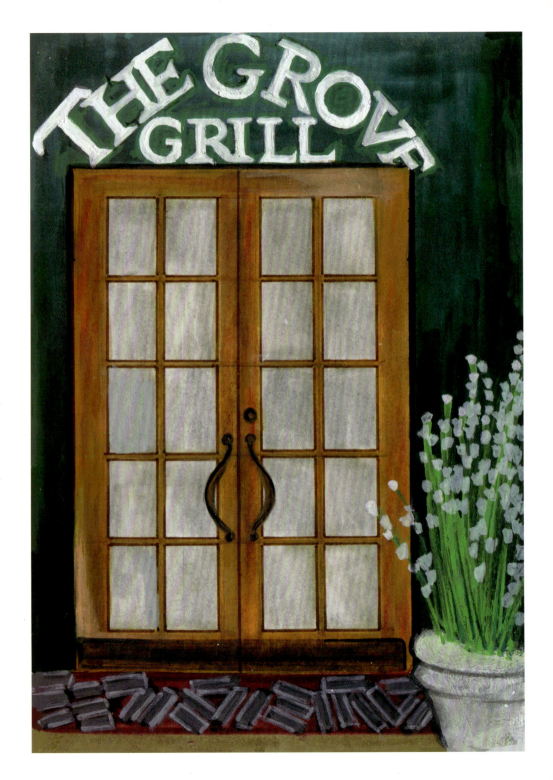

Jambalaya

Ingredient for Creole Tomato Sauce:

½ cup yellow onion, small diced
½ cup green bell pepper, small diced
1 Tablespoon minced garlic, ½ for sauce and ½ for pasta
½ cup chicken stock
1 (14.5-oz.) can diced tomatoes
1 teaspoon freshly chopped thyme leaves
1 teaspoon freshly chopped parsley
¼ teaspoon ground cumin
¼ cup ground coriander
¼ teaspoon ground nutmeg
1 Tablespoon hot sauce, Louisiana sauce works well
2 Tablespoons Worcestershire Sauce
2 oz. red wine
4 Tablespoons tomato paste

Ingredients for Pasta:

Salt for pasta cooking water plus ¾ teaspoon, divided
1 pound dry penne rigate or orzo, both work well
3 Tablespoons olive oil, divided
1 pound peeled, deveined large shrimp
2 Tablespoons plus 1 teaspoon Cajun Spice, use your favorite
¾ pound crawfish tail meat
¾ pound andouille sausage, diced into ½-inch pieces
1 cup Cajun mirepoix: ⅓ each, by volume, small diced onion, bell pepper, and celery
½ cup white wine
½ cup chicken stock

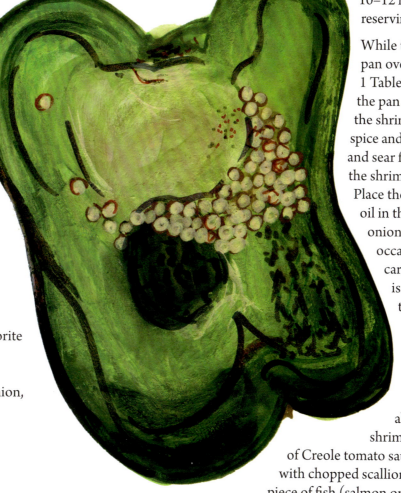

Preparation:

Sauté onion, pepper, and garlic in 1 Tablespoon olive oil, add remaining ingredients, simmer 30 minutes, and blend. Fill a large, 1-gallon stock pot with a pasta insert, ¾ full with water. Bring to a boil over high heat, and season with salt to taste. Place the penne in the salted water, and return to a boil, stirring occasionally. Cook the pasta until nearly al dente, 10–12 minutes. Drain and set aside, reserving 1 cup of the pasta cooking water.

While the pasta cooks, set a large sauté pan over medium-high heat, add 1 Tablespoon of the olive oil, and swirl the pan to evenly coat with the oil. Season the shrimp with 2 teaspoons of Cajun spice and salt. Place the shrimp in the pan, and sear for 1 minute per side. Remove the shrimp from the pan, and set aside. Place the remaining Tablespoon of olive oil in the sauté pan, and add the sausage, onions, and bell peppers. Sauté, stirring occasionally, until the sausage is lightly caramelized and the Cajun mirepiox is translucent, about 3 minutes. Add the garlic to the pan, and sauté for 30 seconds. Add white wine and the chicken stock to the pan, and scrape with a spoon to remove any browned bits that have formed in the bottom of the pan, about 30 seconds. Add crawfish, shrimp, and pasta, and desired amount of Creole tomato sauce. Heat thoroughly. Garnish with chopped scallions. You may also blacken or grill a piece of fish (salmon or grouper work well) on top for a heartier dish.

Hog & Hominy

707 West Brookhaven Circle   901.207.7396

One Prized Pig

Since opening in 2011, Hog & Hominy has enjoyed numerous accolades and is consistently recognized for its innovative blend of Italian and Southern fare. The Biscuit Gnocchi comes to mind. There's nothing ordinary about this place. Not exactly quiet, Hog & Hominy is lively and high energy. A perfect spot to sit back and enjoy sporting events on TV or meet friends at the on-site Bocce court. Now, about the food... Pizza is known as the "Patriarch" here, but I, for one, am taken with some of the other offerings. The Bibb Lettuce Salad of gorgonzola, plums, hazelnuts, and Calabrian chiles is off-the-charts. Each bite of the Shrimp and Grits tastes even better than the bite before. In the end, if you can manage to hold back and save room for dessert, the Peanut Butter Pie is phenomenal.

Spaghetti Squash Marinara

Ingredients:

2 whole spaghetti squashes, about 3½ pounds each
Kosher salt and freshly ground black pepper
1 cup extra-virgin olive oil
8 sprigs fresh thyme
2 cups marinara sauce
8 oz. buffalo mozzarella cheese
Chili oil for drizzling

Preparation:

Preheat the oven to 450 degrees. Cut each squash in half lengthwise, and scoop out the seeds with a sturdy spoon. Arrange the squash halves cut-side up on a rimmed baking sheet. Season them lightly with salt and pepper, drizzle with the olive oil, and top each half with 2 thyme sprigs. Roast the squash halves until fork-tender, about 30 minutes. Remove the squash halves from the oven, and discard the thyme. Fill the squash cavities nearly to the top with marinara. Using your fingers, pull apart the mozzarella into chunks, and scatter them on top of the marinara. Return the squash to the oven, and roast until the marinara starts to bubble and cheese is melted, about 5 more minutes. Remove from the oven, and drizzle with chili oil. Carefully transfer the squash halves to plates, and serve. Serves 4.

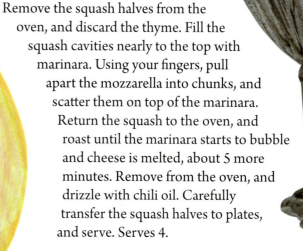

Silver Wine Goblet from Social

Interim

5040 Sanderlin Suite 105   901.818.0821

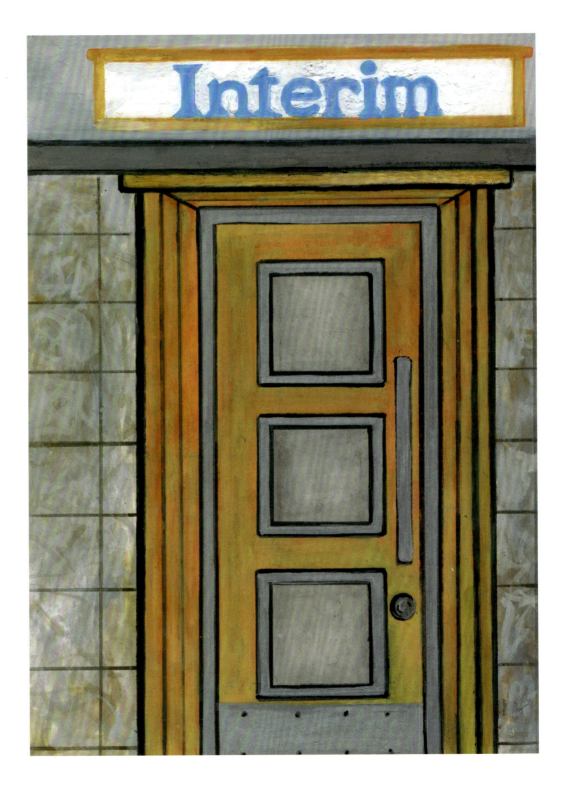

Enjoy The Show

At Interim, a state-of-the-art open kitchen will have you mesmerized watching the steady parade of mouth-watering creations. As an opening number, the Crispy Oysters with arugula, baby carrots, and whole grain mustard aioli steals the show. Everything is impeccably fresh and flavorful. Executive Chef David Krog has masterfully crafted dishes such as Boudin Stuffed Quail, Chicken Breast, and the very popular Braised Lamb Shank. Krog and Franck Oysel, the only French pastry chef in the Mid-South, will see to it that your taste buds have a field day. L' Aegina Pistachio Coulis and Chocolate Decoration is a scrumptious show-stopper. The bustling open kitchen complements a lovely atmosphere with pristine white tablecloths and fresh flowers throughout. And, yes, it is true—the Mac and Cheese Casserole at Interim continues to live up to its phenomenal reputation.

Braised Lamb Shanks

Ingredients:

4 lamb shanks
Salt, enough to completely cover the shanks
10 cloves minced garlic
3 Tablespoons thyme
2 carrots, peeled and sliced
2 onions, peeled and sliced
5 stalks celery, chopped
3 Tablespoons minced garlic
1 bay leaf
1 Tablespoon tomato paste
1 quart red wine
Salt to taste

Preparation:

Use your knife to take off the thick fat from the shanks. It may be easier to buy them pre-cleaned, if possible. Prepare the cure mixture by combining the salt, 10 cloves of minced garlic, and 3 Tablespoons of thyme together. (Curing is the addition to meats of some combination of salt and sugar, for the purpose of preservation, flavor, and color.) Completely cover the shanks with the cure mixture. Wrap and refrigerate for 24 hours. When cure process is complete, thoroughly rinse the shanks under water, and then let dry in the refrigerator.

When the shanks are dried, in a braising pan or large pot, brown all sides of the shanks. Remove the shanks, and set aside. Discard half of the oil in the pan. Into the oil, add the peeled and sliced carrots, onions, and celery. Saute the vegetables until tender. Add the 3 Tablespoons of minced garlic and bay leaf. Sauté briefly. (Don't burn the garlic.) Add tomato paste, and cook with the vegetables. Once the paste covers all the vegetables, add the red wine. Reduce until the liquid thickens. Add the shanks to the pot, and top with water and salt. Bring to a boil. Reduce the heat, and cover. Cook until tender, about 5 hours.

Itta Bena

145 Beale   901.578.3031

Ode to Home

Up the fire escape above the famous B.B. King's Blues Club, on the third floor lies Memphis' "Hidden Gem," Itta Bena. Named for the town where Blues legend B.B. King was born, it features Southern contemporary cuisine inspired by the flavors of the Mississippi Delta. The many scrumptious selections include Crispy Cornmeal Green Tomatoes, Jambalaya Pasta, Jumbo Shrimp and Grits, Duck and Waffles, and Bone-In 16 oz. Ribeye with an option to add Grilled Jumbo Shrimp or Seared Jumbo Scallops. End your meal with White Chocolate Bread Pudding with Golden Raisin Caramel Sauce. If the mood strikes, you can't go wrong with a Blueberry Lemon Drop Martini or a Chocolate Martini. Whew! Classy, jazzy, and romantic this blue oasis overlooks the Atlantic. JUST kidding. Overlooking the historic Beale Street—even better!

Abita BBQ Shrimp

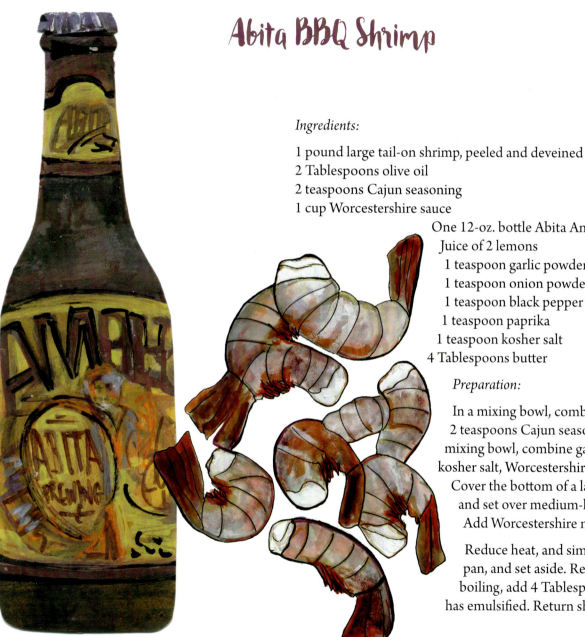

Ingredients:

1 pound large tail-on shrimp, peeled and deveined
2 Tablespoons olive oil
2 teaspoons Cajun seasoning
1 cup Worcestershire sauce
One 12-oz. bottle Abita Amber beer
Juice of 2 lemons
1 teaspoon garlic powder
1 teaspoon onion powder
1 teaspoon black pepper
1 teaspoon paprika
1 teaspoon kosher salt
4 Tablespoons butter

Preparation:

In a mixing bowl, combine shrimp, 1 teaspoon olive oil, and 2 teaspoons Cajun seasoning, and mix until shrimp are coated. In another mixing bowl, combine garlic powder, onion powder, black pepper, paprika, kosher salt, Worcestershire, beer, and lemon juice, and whisk until incorporated. Cover the bottom of a large sauté pan with remaining 1 Tablespoon olive oil, and set over medium-high heat. Once hot, add shrimp, and sauté 2–3 minutes. Add Worcestershire mixture, and bring to a boil.

Reduce heat, and simmer an additional 2–4 minutes. Remove shrimp from pan, and set aside. Return Worcestershire sauce mixture to a boil. Once boiling, add 4 Tablespoons butter, and remove from heat. Whisk until butter has emulsified. Return shrimp to pan, and coat with sauce.

Jim's Place

518 Perkins Extended   901.766.2030

A Family Tradition

Jim's Place has been showcasing the Taras family's warm hospitality and exquisite culinary skills for three generations. A dining tradition in Memphis since 1921, Jim's Place has moved several times, but the Taras' commitment to quality has not wavered. To begin, Dimitri's Charcoal Grilled Jumbo Shrimp basted with Grecian lemon-oregano sauce, the Phyllo Puffs, Bruschetta, or Souflima, will have you drooling for more. All are original family recipes. Steaks charcoal-grilled at Jim's Place are extremely flavorsome. Whether it is Filet Mignon or a Ribeye, steaks at Jim's Place have been popular for a very long time. For me, house favorites like the Chopped Sirloin Southern Style and Grilled Calf's Liver, Southern or Grecian Style, are stunning. Flavors will forever be the front runners here. For dessert—what else? Baklava! Always a winner.

Avocado Soup

Ingredients:

4 Tablespoons butter
4 Tablespoons flour
2 cups milk
2 cups cream of half-and-half
3 avocados
Grated rind of one orange
Salt to taste

Preparation:

Melt butter, add flour. Cook until bubbly. Gradually add milk and cream. Cook until thickened and smooth. Peel and mash 2½ avocados. Add to cream sauce with orange rind. Put in electric blender or food processor, and blend until smooth as velvet. Chill. Serve very cold with reserved avocado on top and sour cream, if you like, with grated orange peel.

Pan-Seared Chilean Sea Bass with Wild Mushroom Grits and Fresh Spinach

Ingredients:

Four 6-oz. center cut fillets Chilean sea bass
Salt and pepper
4 Tablespoons canola oil
1 bunch fresh thyme
6 Tablespoons butter
2 pints assorted mushrooms (shiitake, cremini, Portobello)
2 cups instant grits
1 quart chicken stock
¼ cup heavy cream
1 pound baby spinach, carefully washed

Preparation:

Season the sea bass with salt and pepper. In a large sauté pan over medium heat, add the canola oil, and heat the oil to a slight smoke. Add 1 sprig thyme to the pan, and sear the sea bass skin-side down for ¾ of the cooking time, about 7 minutes. This will give the fish a beautiful crisp skin and golden color. While the fish is cooking, start the grits. In a 2-quart saucepan, add 2 Tablespoons butter and 1 sprig thyme. When the butter begins to brown, add the mushrooms, and sauté until golden. Using a wooden spoon, stir the grits, add the chicken stock, and reduce to a simmer. When the grits begin to thicken, finish with heavy cream and 1 Tablespoon butter. Season with salt and pepper. When ready to serve, remove thyme sprig. Keep grits warm on a low temperature.

Carefully turn the fish over to finish the other side. Remove the sea bass, and hold in a warm place. In the same sauté pan on the same temperature, add the spinach. It will quickly wilt. Finish the spinach with the remaining butter, and season with salt and pepper. For presentation, serve this dish in a large soup bowl. Using a ladle, scoop a small amount of grits into the bottom of each bowl. Layer a small amount of spinach on the grits, and finish with the sea bass. Garnish with fresh thyme.

The Kitchen

415 Great View Drive East 901.729.9009

Leisurely Treat

A beautiful, tranquil setting like no other. I will try to describe it, but I might need your help. They say a picture is worth a thousand words. In the case of the Kitchen at Shelby Farms, they could be right. I do not know when I have seen such a sight. Hyde Lake is stunning, substantial, and so sublime. It does not stop there. Come on inside for a big surprise. Creative dishes to exalt culinary wishes: Let the snacks, starters, and any side be your guide. Pickled Gulf Shrimp, Charred Edamame, Braised Greens with Chili Vinegar, Summer Melon and Country Ham, and Cucumbers and Dill. Some dishes are seasonal, of course. If you have a hearty appetite, try main courses Pasta Bolognese or the Pan Roasted Ribeye. For dessert, the Sticky Toffee Pudding or Peach Cobbler are both world-class.

Mushrooms on Toast

Ingredients:

1 cup crimini mushrooms, roasted
1 Tablespoon thyme, tarragon, chives, and parsley, roughly chopped
2 Tablespoons butter
3 Tablespoons cream
Sherry vinegar
Salt
Pepper

Preparation:

Sauté mushrooms in butter. Add the cream, and reduce until the cream has coated the mushrooms. Add herbs, salt, and pepper to taste. Finish with sherry vinegar. Serve over grilled bread.

Peach Cobbler with Cream

This cobbler is delicious when peaches are in season! It is also a very adaptable recipe in that you can exchange any in-season fruit for the peaches.

Ingredients for Filling:

10 ripe peaches
Juice of 1 orange
½–¾ cup sugar

Ingredients for Crust:

2 cups flour
3 Tablespoons sugar
1 teaspoon baking powder
1 teaspoon baking soda
¼ teaspoon salt
Zest of one lemon
Zest of one orange
1¼ cup cold buttermilk
4 oz. olive oil

2 Tablespoons "Sugar in the Raw" for dusting tops

Preparation:

For the filling, peel and cut the peaches into quarters. Toss in the sugar and orange juice, let macerate, and then begin the crumble topping. Sift all dry ingredients together. Add in the zests, and loosely combine the liquids with the dry ingredients. Mix until just incorporated. Find a baking dish about 12" x 9" and fill the bottom with peaches. With a spoon, spread the topping, making an even layer over the top. Bake at 325 degrees for about 25–30 minutes until golden brown. Once finished, you can top with heavy cream or crème fraîche, and serve.

Las Tortugas Deli Mexicana

1215 South Germantown Rd.   901.751.1200

The Secret's Out

I am not sure tourists are aware of Las Tortugas Deli, but you can bet your bottom dollar (or should I say peso?) that it is no secret for locals! If you are looking for Classic Mexican Cuisine, 100% fresh, authentic, and super tasty. . . this one's for you. Owner Jonathan Magallanes is very passionate about consistency and does not let up. If the choices overwhelm you, let Jonathan decide. Here is a small sampling: De Carnitas Mexico City (Braised Mexican Pork Barbeque Shoulder), De Huachinango Veracruz (Grilled Red Snapper/Tilapia Fillets), De Filet Mignon (Grilled Filet Mignon), and Flaute de Pollo (Deep Fried Chicken Flaute). The Guacamole Verdadero is a must. Delicioso!

King Crab and Gulf Shrimp Cocktail

Ingredients:

3 Alaskan King Crab Legs
24 Gulf shrimp
1 head romaine lettuce
2 cups ketchup
3 limes, juiced
½ small onion, finely chopped
2 avocados, roughly chopped
1 bunch cilantro, leaves only
2 Tablespoons chipotle puree
2 Tablespoons Tabasco sauce
2 Tablespoons red wine vinegar
3 sliced radishes
½ cup shredded lettuce
½ cup finely shredded cabbage
Ritz Crackers

Preparation:

Thaw shrimp, and cook in boiling water. Peel and chill. Refrigerate. Thaw crab legs. Shell and clean crab legs, chill. Cover bottom of martini or cocktail glass with 3–4 leaves of romaine. Place shredded cabbage/lettuce mixture in the bottom of the glass. Season with lime and salt. Combine ketchup, lime juice, vinegar, onion, avocado, cilantro, chipotle, and Tabasco in a glass bowl to make cocktail sauce. Place cocktail sauce over lettuce/cabbage mixture, and top with shrimp and then crab. Garnish with sliced radishes. Serve with crackers on the side. Serves 6.

The Little Tea Shop

69 Monroe   901.525.6000

The Verdict Is In

The jury has spoken at this downtown institution popular with the legal crowd. . . the Little Tea Shop's famous Cornbread Sticks are out of this world! On any given weekday, you may be sitting next to a Who's Who in Memphis at this unassuming restaurant with an impressive list of regulars. Owner Sue prepares wonderful Southern dishes fresh every day. Always on the menu are the famous Lacy Special, a Bowl of Turnip Greens and Couscous Salad with either Grilled Salmon or Grilled Chicken, and memorable salads and sandwiches. Daily specials range from Salmon Croquettes and Baked Moroccan Chicken to Beef and Noodles and Corned Beef and Cabbage. Sue and her crew serve attorneys and a few celebrities here and there, but their heart is open to everyone. And speaking of heart, my darling granddaughter, Lucille, visited at only three weeks old. She had a lovely time. . . slept peacefully through our entire meal.

White Bean Soup

Ingredients:

1 pound white Northern beans
3 quarts chicken broth
2 cups chopped onion
½ cup chopped carrots
½ cup chopped leeks
1 cup chopped celery with leaves
2 cloves garlic, pressed
⅛ teaspoon black pepper
¼ cup chopped parsley
Dash Tabasco Sauce
1 Tablespoon olive oil

Preparation:

Soak beans overnight in water to cover. Place beans in 3 quarts chicken broth in a Dutch oven. Bring to a boil, reduce heat, and simmer covered for 2 hours. Add remainder of ingredients (except Tabasco and olive oil), and simmer another hour. Adjust seasoning. At the very end of cooking time, add Tabasco and olive oil. Serves four for a one-dish dinner; six to eight otherwise.

McEwen's on Monroe

120 Monroe   901.527.7085

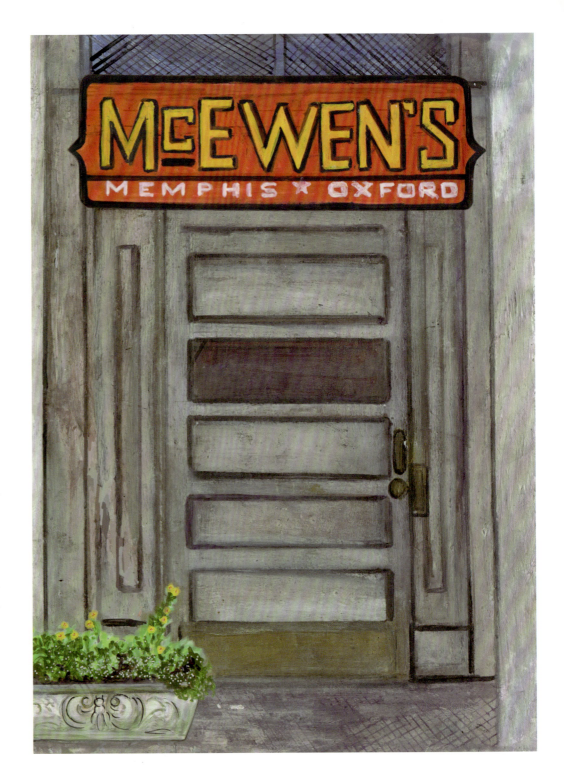

Extraordinary Entrees

What is there to like about McEwen's on Monroe? Everything. What is there not to like? Nothing. With that said, I cannot seem to get away from the Roast Beef Sandwich, red wine jus, horseradish, and provolone baked on a French roll. It has to be the most amazingly flavorful roast beef sandwich in this city. Any side item will accompany, but I choose the Squash Casserole every time. For dinner, where the menu changes seasonally, these dishes are constant: Pan Seared Sea Scallops Piccata Style and Pan Seared Chilean Sea Bass. McEwen's has a wine list to be proud of, embracing boutique vintners. To finish the meal, the Key Lime Pie with homemade whipped cream takes the cake—or should I say the pie? But do ask first, it is not on the menu.

Creole Spiced Braised Pork Osso Buco

Ingredients:

6 portions of pork Osso Buco
Salt and pepper
1 each yellow onion, red bell pepper, and green bell pepper, medium dice
Two 12-oz. cans diced tomatoes, strained
½ bunch celery medium diced
Cajun seasoning
1 bottle white wine
32 oz. apple juice
Veal or beef stock

Preparation:

Tie pork together in butcher's twine. Salt and pepper both sides of pork, and dredge in seasoned flour (salt and pepper). Sear with oil in hot pan on both sides until well browned, and drain excess oil. Add all vegetables to hot pan, and sweat until soft. Season vegetables in Cajun seasoning. Deglaze vegetables with white wine and apple juice. Add pork back to simmering pan. Cover with veal or beef stock. Remove pork, and place in deep baking pan. Pour vegetables and stock to cover. Cover with foil, and bake at 315 degrees for 3–3½ hours. To serve, place pork on your choice of starch, preferably cheddar grits. Pour sauce directly on top of and around pork, and remove string with scissors. As an option, garnish with fried tobacco onions and scallions.

Mesquite Chop House

3165 Forest-Hill Irene   901.249.5661

Ready For Prime Time

To tell it like it is, I have no problem that the focus at Mesquite Chop House is on steaks. The prime filet, rib eyes, and prime aged New York Strip are all utterly delicious. But let's not forget some sensational seafood options. Every evening, on the bar menu only, the luscious Lobster Pizza will put you in LaLa Land. I should also mention the Prime Rib Pizza, consisting of creamed spinach, sliced prime rib, and an artichoke jalapeño relish. It should be on everyone's bucket list. Fresh herbs and vegetables are grown in the back yard of the restaurant. Fresh at Mesquite Chop House cannot be any fresher. Ambience is comfortable, upscale, and spacious. To end your meal, the Vanilla Bean Crème Brulee will more than suffice.

Prime Rib Pizza

Ingredients:

1 corn and flour blend tortilla
3 oz. artichoke hearts
1 oz. pickled jalapeño peppers
½–1 cup Gouda Alfredo sauce
2–3 cups fresh spinach leaves
4 oz. prime rib
2½ cups shredded sharp cheddar cheese
1 teaspoon blackening seasoning
¼ cup fresh tomato, diced
2 Tablespoons green onion, chopped

Preparation:

If you are using a traditional corn and flour-blend tortilla (you may find them at a Latin foods market), begin by deep frying the tortilla. If using a 12" flour tortilla, begin by baking it at 350–375 degrees until golden brown. Then remove from oven.

Next, sauté the spinach with the Gouda Alfredo sauce. To make the Gouda Alfredo sauce, make a normal Alfredo recipe, and add one to two cups of shredded smoked Gouda to your sauce, and let it melt into the sauce. Once you have sautéed the spinach and sauce, spread it over the tortilla as evenly as possible. Next, rough chop the artichokes and jalapeño peppers, and spread them over the tortilla. Then, chop prime rib into bite-size bits. Strategically place half of the it on the tortilla.

Add the cheddar cheese, and make sure to spread the cheese as close to the edges as possible so they do not burn. Then finish adding the rest of the prime rib. Sprinkle blackening seasoning over the pizza, and bake at 350 degrees until cheese is melted. (Usually about 5–8 minutes in a convection oven.) Pull from the oven, and garnish with fresh tomatoes and green onions.

Napa Café

5101 Sanderlin Suite 122   901.683.0441

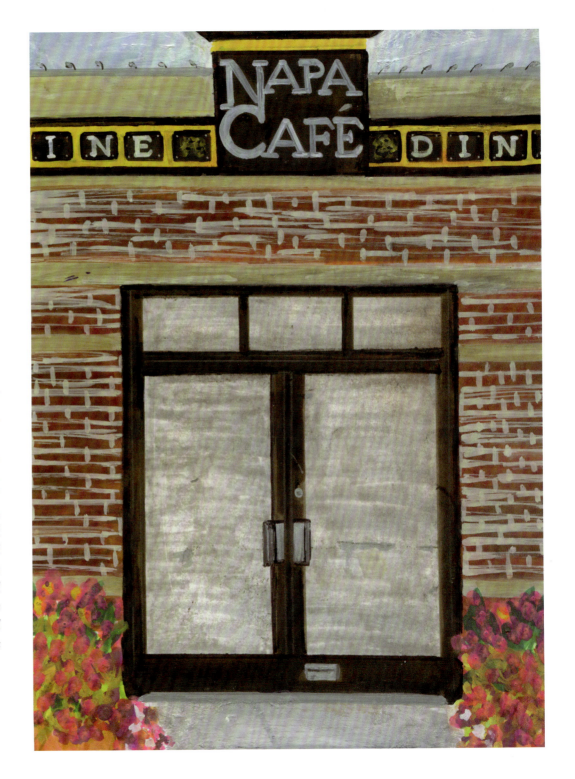

Understated Delight

You have heard of "the perfect lunch place," or the place to "take a date to impress." Well, Napa Café just might be it. Time will tell. Actually, it already has. A popular destination since 1998, Napa Café consistently receives good reviews, including Wine Spectator's Award of Excellence for 12 years in a row. Owner Glenda Hastings does not miss a beat (or beet). Tempting selections for lunch are Grilled Chicken and Avocado Salad, Rosemary Chicken Salad (I love the golden raisins), and the organic Springer Mountain Chicken. Awesome. Dinner, OMG! The Pork Chops and Lamb Specials are serious business. Everything on the menu is better with wines from Napa's thoughtfully selected list, which, of course, includes bottles from the eponymous Napa Valley.

Scallops with Oxtail Dumplings

Ingredients for Oxtail Dumpligs:

1 pound oxtails, braised and deboned, shredded
½ scallion, chopped
½ inch knuckle ginger, minced
Wonton wrappers

Preparation:

Mix oxtail meat, scallion, and ginger together, place in wonton wrappers, and seal.

Ingredients for Sweet Potato Puree:

Cook one large sweet potato, and then peel and puree. Add 1¼ teaspoon ground cumin. Keep warm.

Ingredients for Umami Broth:

2 cups water
1 cup shitake mushrooms
¼ cup parsley stems
2–3 garlic cloves, crushed
1 bay leaf
½ tomato, diced
¼-inch knuckle ginger
¼ pound parmesan cheese
1 sprig each thyme and rosemary
2 cloves garlic
Black pepper, slight turn with pepper mill
1 star anise

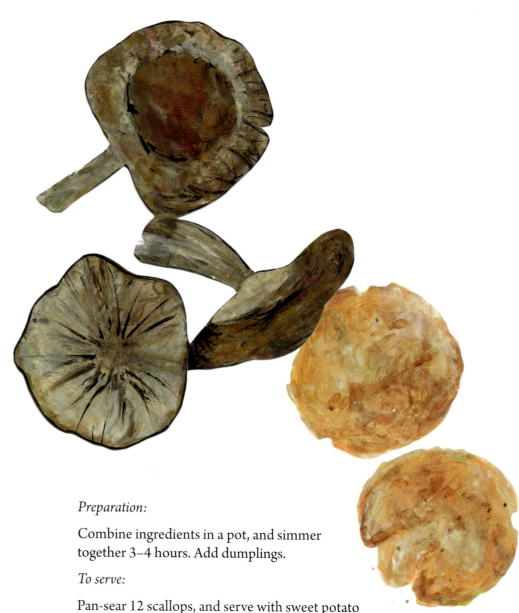

Preparation:

Combine ingredients in a pot, and simmer together 3–4 hours. Add dumplings.

To serve:

Pan-sear 12 scallops, and serve with sweet potato puree, along with oxtail dumplings and steaming broth.

Panda Garden

3735 Summer   901.323.4819

By Golly, She's Right!

Putting your trust in children is not a bad idea. They can be brutally honest. When my five-year-old granddaughter Bays says Panda Garden is the place to go to for Chinese, and to order the Sesame Chicken, she's not kidding. What a smart little girl. And that is not just a proud Grandma talking. Well, maybe a little bragging. Seriously, this unassuming place does not disappoint. Like most Chinese restaurants with a long list of the typical dishes... Spring Rolls, Fried Wontons, Hot & Sour Soup, Wonton Soup, Egg Drop Soup, Fried Rice, Lo Mein, Chow Mein, Chop Suey, Poultry, Pork, Beef, Seafood, and Vegetables... the choices can be overwhelming. Relax. At Panda Garden, anything you order is top-notch, super tasty, and affordable to boot.

Salt 'n' Pepper Shrimp

Ingredients:

50 shrimp
1½ Tablespoon corn flour
Diced green pepper
Diced red pepper
Diced onion
½ Tablespoon black pepper
2 Tablespoons cooking wine
¼ cup chicken stock
1 egg

Preparation:

Shell and devein shrimp. Bread shrimp with corn flour mixed with egg. Lightly fry shrimp for 20 seconds, and then lightly fry peppers and onion for 5 seconds. Drain excess oil, and stir fry all of the above in a wok on high heat with salt, black pepper, cooking wine, and chicken stock for 2 minutes. Serve immediately. Serves 5.

O God , I am as one hungry for rice, parched as one thirsty for tea. Fill my so empty heart. Amen
–Chinese prayer

Paulette's

50 Harbour Town Square   901.260.3300

Tried and True

This charming French/Continental restaurant is very dear to my heart. Many restaurants come and go. Not this one. I have been a huge fan of Paulette's for over 30 years, enjoying dependable awesome cuisine. George Falls, an owner and most gracious host, would not have it any other way. The ambience is quaint and romantic—fresh flowers on every table, most often gorgeous large roses. What to order? Everything! Seriously. You can't go wrong with the Filet Paulette with its pepper-butter sauce or absolutely any crepe on the menu. The Grilled Brochette of Chicken is a staple, one of my favorites. The Lump Crabmeat Stuffed Mushrooms are to die for! The warm popovers served with house-made strawberry butter always hit the spot.

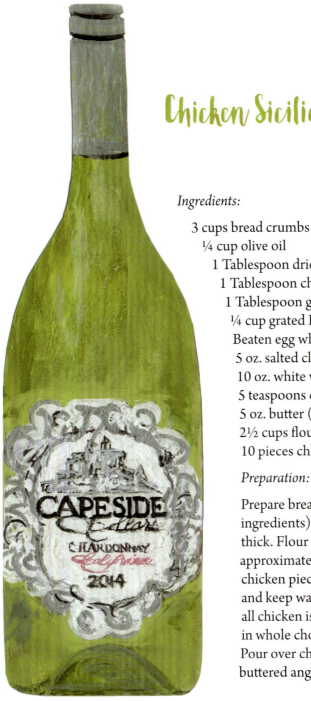

Chicken Sicilian

Ingredients:

- 3 cups bread crumbs
- ¼ cup olive oil
- 1 Tablespoon dried oregano
- 1 Tablespoon chopped parsley
- 1 Tablespoon garlic
- ¼ cup grated Parmesan cheese
- Beaten egg white
- 5 oz. salted clarified butter
- 10 oz. white wine
- 5 teaspoons chopped garlic
- 5 oz. butter (not melted)
- 2½ cups flour
- 10 pieces chicken breast, 3 oz. each

Preparation:

Prepare breading by mixing all breading ingredients together (First six ingredients). Using a meat mallet, pound chicken breast flat, about ¼ inch thick. Flour chicken lightly, dip in beaten egg white, then in breading. Place approximately one ounce of clarified butter in skillet over high heat. Place chicken pieces in pan, and sauté until golden brown. Remove from skillet, and keep warm. Repeat with more clarified butter and chicken pieces until all chicken is cooked. In the same skillet, add white wine and garlic, whisk in whole chopped butter tossed in flour until the sauce has a creamy texture. Pour over chicken breasts, and serve. Serves 10. As an accompaniment, serve buttered angel hair or vermicelli pasta and green beans or broccoli.

Porcellino's Craft Butcher

711 West Brookhaven Circle   901.762.6656

A Talent for Taste

Michael Hudson has come a long way since I met him just over 10 years ago as he was doing his magic in the kitchen of Chez Philippe. Michael and partner Andrew Ticer's third restaurant, Porcellino's Craft Butcher, has taken off like a rocket. There's no stopping this prolific talent. They recently opened Catherine & Mary's at the Chisca on Main and Josephine Estelle at Ace Hotel in New Orleans. Porcellino's originality is astounding. There's a different quiche (always spectacular) offered daily for breakfast or lunch. The Sweet Potato Fries, topped with poblano fonduta, and charred Vidalia onions, are meant to be shared, but you may not want to. Being a butcher shop as well as a restaurant means freshness supersedes all. The never-ending flavors of the bacon and spicy maple sausage are mind-boggling.

Banana Bread

Ingredients:

7 brown bananas (can be frozen then thawed, should yield about 3 cups)
¾ cup butter
3 cups sugar
1½ tablespoon vanilla
3 eggs
1 cup heavy cream
3¾ cup flour or gluten-free flour
3 teaspoon baking powder
3 teaspoon baking soda
1½ teaspoon salt
1½ cup finely chopped walnuts

Preparation:

Preheat the oven to 350 degrees. Mash the bananas into a pureé. Cream together the butter and sugar by whisking or using a stand mixer. Mix in the vanilla, eggs, and cream. Be careful not to overmix, or the bread will slump in the middle. In a separate bowl, sift together the flour, baking powder, baking soda, and salt. Mix these dry ingredients together. Whisk together with the wet ingredients, and add the mashed bananas and walnuts in as well. Mix everything together using a whisk or stand mixer. Mix until no more lumps are evident, but again, be careful not to overmix. Pour the dough into 2 buttered loaf pans, and bake for 50–60 minutes. Makes 2 loaves.

Restaurant Iris

2146 Monroe   901.590.2828

Charming, Romantic, Delicious

In a lovingly restored home tucked behind beautiful landscaping, Restaurant Iris could easily be a Yard of the Month winner in this neighborhood by Overton Square. Restaurant Iris, a haven for French Creole cuisine, is used to winning. Deservedly so. Owner/Chef Kelly English was a James Beard's semi-finalist early in his career, and the accolades have not stopped since. The experience begins with the tantalizing smells that tease you as you approach the entrance. Oh! It's the lovely herb garden hidden on the right. Talk about fresh. Go inside and you'll be enveloped by the romantic ambience. The choices are like no other. I thoroughly enjoyed the Heirloom Tomato Salad with labneh, pine nuts, spring onions, cucumber, and molasses vinaigrette. Rod Bailey's Raviolo with brown butter and mushrooms is marvelous. The New York Strip stuffed with fried oysters and blue cheese is richly intense. Food-lovers nation-wide agree.

Amandine of Redfish and Cauliflower

Ingredients:

Four 7-oz. portions of skin-on redfish
½ cup toasted and sliced almonds
4 Tablespoons chopped parsley
8 Tablespoons whole unsalted butter
8 juiced lemons
1 cup heavy cream
1 head cauliflower (florets removed from body)
Vegetable oil to sear and sauté
Salt to taste
Creole seasoning
  to taste

Preparation:

Blanch the cauliflower florets in slightly salted water at a rolling boil while heating the heavy cream and 2 Tablespoons butter in a separate pot. When cauliflower is tender, strain and slightly dry in a 300 degree oven. Put the dried florets in a blender with the cream and butter mixture, and puree till smooth, and then season with salt. Reserve puree. Season the fish with salt and Creole seasoning. Heat a cast iron pan to medium heat, add the oil, and sear the fish skin side down until crisp, and then flip and cook till done. Remove the fish, and pour off the grease. Put the pan back on the heat, add in the remaining butter, and cook till brown. Add in the almonds, and toss until the nuts brown a little more. Add chopped parsley and lemon juice. Season the sauce with salt. Place a spoonful of cauliflower in the center of a plate, top with the fish, and spoon on the sauce. Serves 4.

The Second Line

2144 Monroe   901.590.2829

Strike Up the Band

If you are looking for a taste of New Orleans, the Second Line is cause for celebration. Conveniently located in Midtown Memphis just off Overton Square, this bustling eatery offers dishes such as Fried Chicken Livers served with hot-pepper jelly, Chicken and Andouille Gumbo (highly recommended by local food and wine connoisseur Hal Lewis), and Po' Boys galore! When the weather is nice, the popular outdoor patio is a happening place. Year-round, there's some serious frying going on here: Fried Gulf Shrimp, Fried Gulf Oysters, and Fried Mississippi Catfish. Vegetarians will enjoy the Mushroom Debris. And, by all means, do not overlook the Red Beans and Rice and especially the Spinach Madeleine. There's a reason Memphis magazine readers continue to vote Chef Kelly English the Best Chef in Memphis.

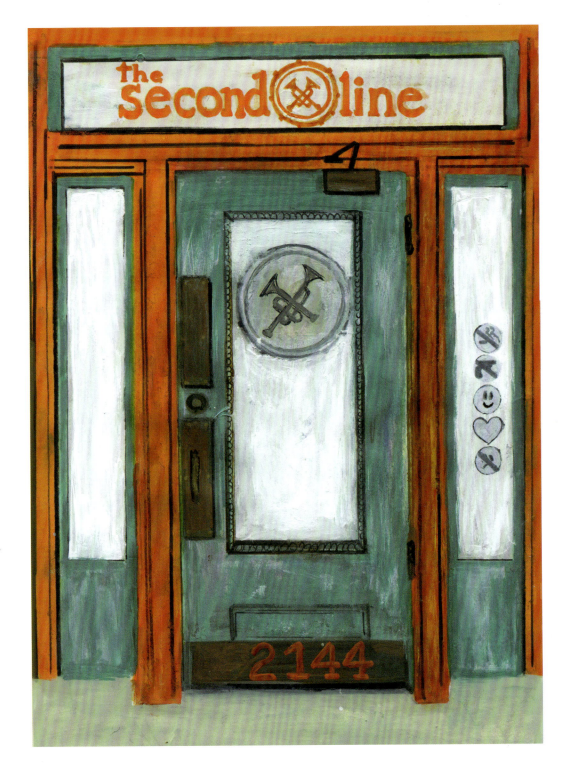

Catfish Sauce Piquant

Ingredients for Sauce Piquant:

1 onion, medium diced
1 bell pepper, medium diced
2 stalks celery, medium diced
2 cloves garlic, minced
2 pounds summer tomatoes, chopped (use canned if out of season)
1 quart chicken stock
½ stick unsalted butter
½ cup flour
1 bay leaf
3 Tablespoons fresh tarragon, roughly chopped
Salt to taste
Cayenne pepper to taste
1 teaspoon ground allspice

Preparation:

Sweat the onion, bell pepper, garlic, and celery in butter. Season with salt and cayenne pepper. Carefully add in flour, and stir to make a blonde roux. Add stock and bay leaf. Cook for 10 minutes on medium heat.
Add all chopped tomatoes. Add tarragon and allspice. Simmer until slightly thickened, and taste
for seasoning.

Ingredients for the catfish:

½ cup canola oil
8 Mississippi catfish filets
½ cup of your favorite Creole seasoning
Green onions to garnish

Preparation:

Season the fish with Creole seasoning and additional salt if your seasoning needs it. Cook fish in a medium-hot cast iron skillet. Serve two filets per serving topped with the sauce and served with rice.
Garnish with green onions.
Serves 4.

South Main Sushi & Grill

520 South Main   901.249.2194

Experienced Newbie

The South Main Sushi & Grill is relatively new to the South Main Arts District Downtown, but the owners' over 40 years of experience are captured in every bite. At this South Main eatery, Japanese cuisine is queen. Express Lunch in a Box… really does rock! Ginger salad, two-piece sashimi, shrimp and vegetable tempura, fried rice, and your choice of Grilled Salmon, Grilled Shrimp, or Beef Julienne. For dinner, the atmosphere entices as lighting enhances the lovely Japanese décor. Entrees are Hibachi Steak, Hibachi Scallops, Chicken Yakisoba Noodle, Twin Lobster Tails, and, believe it or not, Hibachi Chateaubriand. Love it! Happy Hour will truly make you happy. Enjoy very low prices for beer, wine, specialty drinks, and incredibly delicious appetizers.

Crunchy Shrimp Roll

Ingredients:

1 Sushi rolling mat
2 Tablespoons eel sauce
1 dash sesame seed
1 piece Nori dried seaweed
4 oz. cooked sushi rice
1 Tablespoon mayonnaise
1 piece asparagus
2 pieces tempura fried shrimp

Preparation:

Place Nori seaweed shiny side down and horizontal. Take ball of sushi rice, and spread even layer over seaweed. Sushi rice will be sticky; lightly wetting fingertips with water will assist in spreading the rice. Sprinkle sesame seed over rice. Flip seaweed so rice is facing down, then place on top of rolling mat. In the middle of the seaweed, spread thin layer of mayonnaise, then add asparagus and tempura fried shrimp. Using rolling mat, fold up the sushi from the bottom towards middle of the roll, creating a seal. Then continue rolling to the top and shape into a uniform roll. Cut into 8 pieces, drizzle eel sauce on top, and enjoy! Generally served with pickled ginger and wasabi on the side.

Staks Pancake Kitchen

4615 Poplar   901.509.2367

Everyday's A Celebration

Pretty is as pretty does. The Birthday Cake pancake at Staks is as pretty on the inside as it is on the outside. Delectable no less. And it does not even have to be your birthday. Other creative and decadent choices of pancakes are Chocolate Raspberry, Cinnamon Roll, Lemon Ricotta and Buckwheat. Egg dishes are also a big hit: Huevos Rancheros, Breakfast Burritos, and Omelettes, to name a few. Try the Shrimp 'n' Grits— creamy smoked-Gouda grits and shrimp sautéed with mushrooms, spinach, and scallions—all topped with a poached egg. Yum! For lunch Staks offers a variety of soups, salads, and sandwiches, all so inviting. The Pimento Cheese BLT is something to celebrate: homemade pimento cheese, Porcellino's bacon, lettuce, and tomato on sourdough. Staks is great for the entire family. Contemporary and bright. It's good to the last bite.

Lemon Ricotta Pancakes

Ingredients:

¾ cup flour
½ teaspoon baking soda
½ teaspoon salt
1 cup ricotta cheese
2 egg yolks (save the whites)
⅓ cup whole milk
1 teaspoon lemon zest
1½ Tablespoon lemon juice
½ teaspoon vanilla

Preparation:

Mix the first three ingredients. In another bowl, mix ricotta, egg yolks, milk, lemon zest, lemon juice, and vanilla. Add to dry ingredients. Beat the reserved egg whites, and fold into the mixture. Cook pancakes on a hot skillet until done. Top with butter, blueberries, powdered sugar, and blueberry syrup if desired.

Strano! Sicilian Kitchen & Bar

948 South Cooper   901.275.8986

Benvenuto

Welcome to this memorable Sicilian kitchen. As it was in the beginning, it is now and ever shall be, HOT house-made garlic ciabatta bread served with garlic-infused olive oil is most welcoming. And then, who could turn down Grandma's Meatballs? Pesto Cream Gnocchi, rich and heavenly, is out of this world. And it is Sicilian for sure! Salads soar with choices like Fennel all'Arancia, Insalata Caprese, and more. Not surprisingly, the Pizzas here are worthy of standing ovations. But you won't want to miss the Wood-Grilled Pork Tenderloin or the Prosciutto Wrapped Beef Tenderloin. Seven days a week, Strano! at the northeast corner of Cooper and Young, serves superb Sicilian cuisine. Mamma Mia!

Pesto Chicken Gnocchi

Ingredients for Pesto Sauce:

3 cups packed basil
4 garlic cloves
¾ cup Parmesan cheese
½ cup extra virgin olive oil
¼ cup pine nuts
½ cup parsley

Preparation:

Combine all ingredients in the blender until smooth.

Ingredients for Pesto Chicken Gnocchi:

2 oz. red onion
1 artichoke heart
2 oz. sundried tomatoes
2 oz. caramelized onion
2 oz. Roma tomatoes
2 oz. roasted garlic
5 oz. house pesto sauce
3 oz. heavy cream
2 oz. Parmesan cheese
4 oz. grilled chicken

Preparation:

Sauté all ingredients except pesto and cream in olive oil, and then mix in pesto and cream until emulsified. Add fresh grilled chicken and blanched gnocchi. Serve with fresh Parmesan on top.

Benedetto questo cibo–Italian blessing

Sweet Grass

937 South Cooper   901.278.0278

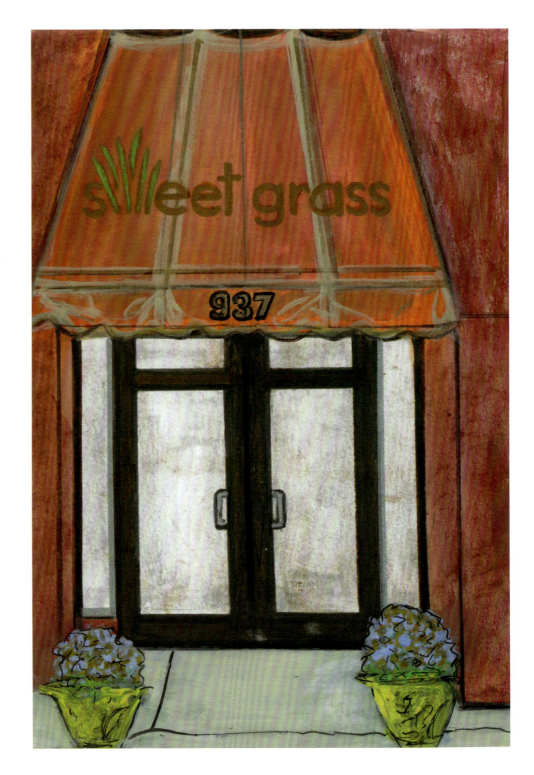

Sweet Déjà vu

Something about this neighborhood bistro serving coastal low country cuisine gave me a sense of déjà vu. Indeed. Having two children that graduated from the College of Charleston, SC, I frequented Slightly North of Broad, unaware that Ryan Trimm was there working under Chef Frank Lee. In 2010, Trimm opened Sweet Grass along with restauranteur Glenn Hays in Memphis. One thing is certain... they don't slack when it comes to snacks: Beef Carpaccio, Steamed Mussels, Fried Oysters and Shrimp. Very tasty. A little more substantial, Oyster Stew, Grilled Pork Breast, Pan Roasted Grouper, and of course, without apologies, Low Country Shrimp & Grits. Sunday night is Prime Rib Night. Go early before they run out. Out of this world—divine! Brunch is very inviting, with such mouth-watering dishes as Banana Bread French Toast and their Fried Green Tomato BLT.

Duck Leg Confit & Grilled Breast with Dirty Brussels Sprouts

Ingredients:

2 duck breasts
2 duck legs

Ingredients for Duck Leg Cure:

3 cups salt
1 cup sugar
2 bay leaves
1 teaspoon cayenne pepper
8 black peppercorns, ground
15 coriander seeds, toasted and ground
1 star anise, toasted and ground
8 cups rendered duck fat

Ingredients for Dirty Brussels Sprouts:

3 Tablespoons diced bacon
3 cups Brussels sprouts, blanched and halved
2 Tablespoons cider vinegar
⅔ cup bleu cheese
½ cup toasted walnuts

Preparation:

Mix all of the cure ingredients together, and allow legs to cure for 7–12 hours. Remove and rinse thoroughly. Submerge in rendered duck fat, and bring to a simmer over medium-low heat. Slowly simmer on stove until duck leg is tender though, or place in a 275 degree oven for about 7 hours until leg is tender. Once cooked, sprinkle a little salt and pepper on the leg, and sear on all sides in a pan with a thin layer of oil.

Render bacon over medium heat. Add Brussels sprouts, and cook to golden. Deglaze with vinegar, and add bleu cheese and walnuts. Season appropriately, and serve under duck leg.

Grill the duck breasts to medium. Allow to rest for 3–5 minutes, slice them, and serve against the leg and Brussels sprouts.

If you bought whole ducks and fabricated them on your own, it is suggested that you roast the bones and make a nice duck stock. Once made and reduced by 75%, sauté a chopped shallot, add a sprig of thyme, and a splash of dry red wine. Reduce until viscous and sauce-like.

Tsunami

928 South Cooper   901.274.2556

A Wave of Pleasure

Wow! Owner/chef Ben Smith's inventive and stunning expressions of Pacific Rim, Asian, Australian, and South Pacific cuisine has locals flocking to Tsunami. Year after year, Tsunami is awarded Best Seafood in Memphis magazine's Readers' Restaurant Poll. Smith serves only pristine fish and the freshest and finest ingredients. The Spinach Salad with ginger-soy vinaigrette and goat cheese is absolutely delightful. In my view, however, it's the Roasted Sea Bass on black Thai rice with soy beurre blanc that steals the show. Over the top. Heavenly. The "small plates," are ever changing and can be very inviting. . . some are not so small. The Roasted Salmon with spinach, walnut, goat cheese-stuffed Portobello mushroom, and sun dried tomato pesto is truly divine.

Pork and Lemongrass Meatballs

Ingredients:

1 pound ground pork
2 shallots, minced
3 cloves garlic, minced
2 Tablespoons chopped lemongrass
¼ cup chopped cilantro
1 egg, lightly beaten
½ cup Panko bread crumbs
1 jalapeño pepper, chopped
1 teaspoon fish sauce
1 teaspoon salt

Preparation:

Mix all ingredients together well. Portion, using a #40 ice cream scoop. Roll into balls and place on a sheet pan. Refrigerate for at least an hour before cooking. To cook, first dredge in seasoned flour with plenty of fresh ground black pepper, then cook until golden brown on all sides and cooked through.

Wasabi Deviled Eggs

Ingredients:

12 eggs
2 tablespoons wasabi powder
2 tablespoons water
1½ teaspoons mushroom soy
1 cup mayonnaise

Preparation:

Mix the wasabi powder and water to make a smooth paste. Cover and set aside for later.

Place the eggs in an even layer in a saucepan. Add enough cold water to cover. Bring to a boil on high heat. Cover the pan, remove from the heat, and allow the eggs to sit in the hot water for 15 minutes. Drain and cool the eggs.

When cool, peel and cut in half lengthwise. Grate the yolks on the small holes of a box grater, or push them through a fine sieve.

Mix together the wasabi paste, the mushroom soy, and the mayonnaise. Place in a piping bag or a ziplock bag with the corner cut out, and portion equally into all of the egg halves. Before serving, garnish each egg with a sprinkling of furikake, preferably *katsuo fumi* furikake.

The Woman's Exchange

88 Racine   901.327.5681

Labor of Love

As a child I frequented the Tea Room at the Woman's Exchange with my mother. She was a member of the Woman's Exchange. At the time, daughters and granddaughters of members came in once a month to decorate sacks and boxes for gift items. We were paid generously with yummy finger sandwiches and cookies. The Woman's Exchange of Memphis was founded in 1885 as a nonprofit organization offering handmade clothing, toys, linens, and gift items made by local artists. The Tea Room opened in 1962. And so it began... depending on the day of the week, choices include turnip greens, yams, catfish, beef tenderloin, and corn soup. Rev's Meat Loaf is served most every Tuesday, and his Famous Chicken Spaghetti Fiesta is on the menu daily in the summer. From the heavenly fare in the Tea Room to the delicate baby items, everything at the Woman's Exchange is made with love.

Chicken with Artichokes

Ingredients:

3 boneless skinless chicken breasts, diced
1½ medium onions, diced
2½ cups rice, cook per package instructions
2 cans artichoke hearts, drained and chopped
2 teaspoons salt
1 teaspoon pepper
1 Tablespoon mayonnaise
1 can cream of chicken soup

Preparation:

Preheat oven to 325 degrees. Place rice in a large, oblong baking dish. Then add chicken, artichokes, onions, salt, and pepper. Mix mayonnaise and cream of chicken soup together thoroughly, and pour over all. Bake uncovered for 35–40 minutes. Serves 8.

Seafood Charleston

Ingredients:

½ cup butter
1½ cup milk
3 Tablespoons flour
½ teaspoons salt
1 cup onion, minced
¼ green pepper, minced
One 2-oz. jar chopped pimento, drained
1 Tablespoon butter
2 Tablespoons Worcestershire sauce
2 egg yolks, beaten
¾ cup heavy cream
1 cup mushrooms, sliced and sautéed
1½ pounds shrimp. Cooked and cleaned, *or*
1 pound crab meat or lobster, cooked

Preparation:

Cook ½ cup butter, milk, flour, and salt in top of a double boiler over boiling water until thick. Saure onion, pepper, and pimento for 5 minutes in 1 Tablespoon butter. Combine mixtures in double boiler, and add Worcestershire sauce. Just before serving, add egg yolks and cream slowly. Reheat, but do not boil. Add mushrooms and the seafood of your choice. Serves 8. May be served over curried rice or in a ramekin.

P.S. Two from the past...

I have a fascination and admiration with the great French chef Fernand Point (1897-1955). My newest friend did not know me... nor did I him. But on a whim, I found his book, and I am hooked. As are Charlie Trotter, Thomas Keller, and Brown Burch to name a few. Fernand Point is considered to be the father of modern French cuisine. His cookbook, *Ma Gastronomie*, first published in 1969 in French and in 1974 in English, is regarded by many chefs as a gastronomic bible.

A few of Fernand's quotes I will share. It's only fair:

"One distinguishes a good cuisiner by his sauces."

"In the orchestra of a la grande cuisine, the saucier is a soloist."

"Wines that are too old are not suitable for cooking. Fire cannot give them back the strength they have lost."

"I like to start my day of with a glass of champagne. I like to wind up with champagne, too. To be frank, I also like a glass or two in between."

"Butter! Give me Butter! Always Butter!"

A Treasured Find

The stately 19th century mansion at 1085 Poplar, currently home to the Memphis Child Advocacy Center, was originally a private home. In 1958, it was transformed into the Four Flames, an elegant restaurant patronized by Memphis' elite. Even Elvis Presley dined there. The Oysters Harlan appetizer was a favorite among many.

Four Flames Oysters Harlon

Ingredients:

24 fresh shelled oysters
Salt and pepper to taste
Flour for coating
2 Tablespoons fresh lemon juice
1 cup A1 Steak Sauce
2 Tablespoons Worcestershire Sauce
2 jiggers sherry or Madeira
2 Tablespoons flour
3 Tablespoons water

Preparation:

Salt and pepper oysters, and dredge in flour. Grill them on a lightly buttered grill, or sauté lightly in a heavy skillet until browned on both sides. Set aside, and keep warm. Heat in a saucepan without boiling, the lemon juice, A1 Sauce, Worcestershire Sauce, and sherry. Blend the 2 Tablespoons of flour with water, and add to sauce to thicken. Place oysters on a platter, and pour about a spoonful of sauce on each one. Run the platter briefly under the broiler to brown before serving.

Best Sweets: Seven from Heaven

Go ahead and take a seat. Daring, decadent and bold.
No standing you've been told.
Candy, cake, and pie. No time or reason in being shy.
It's just that good... Dive in—it is no sin!

Coconut Cake– Cafe Palladio on Central Avenue
Coconut cake, for goodness sake... VERY moist yellow cake topped with white icing and tender juicy grated coconut.

Fruit Flavored Ice Chips– Dinstuhl's Fine Candies on Grove Park, Pleasant View or Poplar. Orange, Lime, Lemon, and Strawberry

Jake's Original Hot Fudge Pie– Westy's on North Main
Hot fudge pie topped with French vanilla ice cream, Hershey's chocolate syrup, and whipped cream.

Orange Olive Oil Cake– Bluff City Coffee on Main
An Italian cake that has no icing... clearly enticing!

Orange Vanilla Pop– Mempops on Ridgeway Road
Much like the old fashioned Dreamsicle... fresh-squeezed orange juice, cream, and vanilla syrup.

Frankly Scarlet Cupcake– Muddy's Bake Shop on Sanderlin or South Cooper. A red velvet cupcake with cream cheese icing.

Caramel Brownie– Good Caramel Karma at Woman's Exchange Tea Room on Racine. This celestial caramel brownie available on Thursdays only.

Delta Blues Winery

6585 Stewart Road, Lakeland, TN   901.829.46851

Cheers!

After driving down the long winding road of Stewart, not too far from Highway 70, you might think you are in Sonoma or Napa Valley. Actually, you are in Lakeland, Tennessee at Delta Blues Winery. Get ready for fun, music and song—and tasting delightful wines. Bringing your own picnic is encouraged but note that cheese, sausage, crackers, gourmet jellies and sauces are also available. If you are really lucky, Sheila Wilson's way-over-the-top grilled cheese with chocolate will be offered. Heavenly! And so are the beautiful grounds.

english vintage cork screw hand made from grape vine

The Delta Grilled Cheese

This is good as an appetizer with any red wine, especially with the Delta Red from Delta Blues Winery, Lakeland, Tennessee, or just to have as a late night snack.

Ingredients:

16 slices white bread
1 pound Sweetwater Buttermilk Cheese
1 stick softened butter
Dark chocolate, 60 % Cacao, melted

Here's to the corkscrew—a useful key to unlock the storehouse of wit, the treasury of laughter, the front door of fellowship, and the gate of pleasant folly.

–W.E.P. French

Preparation:

Cut crusts off bread, and spread small amount of butter on both sides. Cut and place cheese between two pieces of buttered bread, and then place the sandwich in a hot skillet. Let the bread brown, and turn over and brown the other side. Right before taking out of skillet, using a spatula, slightly flatten the sandwich. Take out of skillet, and cut diagonally, creating a triangle. Drizzle the melted chocolate on top of the triangle, and serve with a glass of red wine. Makes 8 sandwiches.

Bardog Tavern
73 Monroe   901.275.8752

Sit. Stay.

If you are looking for typical bar food, you would be in the wrong place. Bardog Tavern daily specials range from Pork Tenderloin Sope with achiote, to Chorizo Patty Melt or Mussels. The tantalizing Tomato Bisque is on the menu always. Owner Aldo Dean's Italian heritage shines through in generous portions of their much sought after Spaghetti with Marinara or with NJ Meatballs. The Penne alla Vodka is another crowd pleaser. My favorite is the Mother Clucker sandwich, with pepper jack, lettuce, tomato, onion, roasted red pepper and spicy mayo. I run to fetch it almost every week!

Bardog Tavern Vodka Penne

Ingredients:

1 serving cooked penne pasta
1 Tablespoon olive oil
¼ teaspoon minced garlic
Five peeled shrimp, 16/20 size, or chicken
Salt and pepper
Pinch red pepper flakes
1½ oz. vodka
6–8 oz. marinara sauce
½ oz. grated parmesan
½–1 oz. heavy cream

Preparation:

Heat olive oil in sauté pan. Add minced garlic to pan. Add shrimp or chicken with salt and pepper, and toss until cooked. Add red pepper flakes, then add vodka. (Be careful, as vodka will flame.) When vodka has cooked off, add marinara, parmesan, and heavy cream. Then add cooked penne. Toss, adding more parmesan if desired.

2559 Broad   901.730.0719

The Cove

Smooth Sailin' Here

The Cove is all about atmosphere, atmosphere, atmosphere. Warm, inviting, and fun. This nautically themed bar is like no other. Retro vinyl red booths and magnificent chandeliers surrounded by paintings of "early sailors." The Cove is known as a late-night bar with live music and good food. Go early and enjoy a quiet meal or go later and eat to a louder beat—if you can find a seat. The salads, panini, or pizza will not disappoint, but the Oyster Sampler is awesome. Two raw, two Casino, two Rockefeller, and two Blue Cheese oysters. All impeccably fresh.

Rockefeller Spinach and Artichoke Dip

Ingredients:

2 cups Rock sauce
½ cup cream chesse
½ cup 50/50 grated pizza cheese
6 artichokes, coarsely chopped
½ tsp garlic powder

Preparation:

Place all ingredients in a bowl, and mix well. Put in a casserole dish, and lightly dust with cayenne powder. This can be refrigerated until needed. Heat in a 400 degree oven for 20–25 minutes.

Rockefeller Sauce

Ingredients:

5 pounds spinach
3 large yellow onions
4 celery stalks
3 bunches washed Italian (flat) parsley
3 sticks butter
2 teaspoons salt
¾ teaspoon black pepper
3 Tablespoons thyme
½ teaspoon cayenne pepper
2½ teaspoons Worcestershire
2¼ cups bread crumbs
½ cup Herbsaint anise-flavored liquor

Preparation:

Cook spinach, onions, celery, and parsley, and press out all the water and liquid. Process all in a food processor. Put the chopped vegetables in a pot with butter, and simmer for 1½ hours. Add all the other ingredients, and then stir in Herbsaint, and simmer for 20 minutes. (The Cove freezes the sauce in baggies and takes it out as needed for oysters and dip.)

The 5 Spot

84 GE Patterson   901.523.9754

The Flavor is Spot On

The late Russell George has many fans; they will not have 5 Spot go to pot. It started out at the back of the inimitable Ernestine & Hazel's. It was extremely small, serving surprisingly good fare. Today it is much larger, with indoor and outdoor seating. The quaint bar accommodates lovely jewels, and maybe a few drunken fools, with a hip and sassy menu. Creative selections include: Bacon Mac and Cheese Eggroll, 16-oz. Ribeye with Chimichurri Sauce, Braised Oxtail Tacos, and Willie T's Skillet Shrimp. And don't forget Monsieur Jacques de Pirtle—described as a big ass double decker BLT with Jack Pirtle fried chicken skins and bacon. Devilishly delish!

Monsieur Jacques de Pirtle BLT

Ingredients:

3 slices Texas toast
Duke's mayonnaise
3 slices bacon
Iceberg lettuce
Sliced, seasoned tomatoes
Two seasoned and fried chicken skins

Preparation:

Take three slices of Texas toast and butter the two outside pieces, and then toast or grill. Build the sandwich from the bottom up. Place one piece of toast grilled side down. Spread with Duke's mayonnaise. Break three slices of bacon in half, and place across this piece of toast. Place untoasted middle of bread on top of bacon, and spread top side with Duke's. Layer iceberg lettuce, and then sliced, seasoned tomatoes (salted and peppered) on top of lettuce. Arrange two seasoned and fried chicken skins on the tomato layer, and top with last piece of toasted bread.

Cut the sandwich in two, and place a frill pick in each half to keep sandwich from sliding apart. Place on deli paper on a rectangular tin plate.

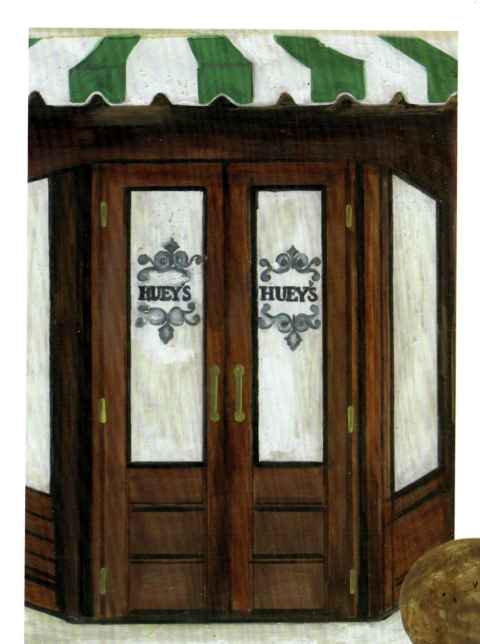

Huey's 1927 Madison 901.726.4372

Burger Heaven

I remember Huey's from the early days—the Union Avenue location in the early '70's. Even then, they served the best hamburger this side of heaven. They've had rave reviews ever since. The meat came from the old John Gray Grocery on Madison Avenue (now closed). Founded in 1970 by Alan Gary, Huey's was known more as a bar. Today it's a full-blown restaurant, a Memphis institution with seven locations thanks to Thomas Boggs, who purchased it in 1976 and took it to a higher level. Huey's has been voted "Best Burger" in the Memphis *magazine's Readers' Restaurant Poll 31 years in a row.*

Potato Soup

Ingredients:

¼ bunch celery, diced
¾ cup diced onions
1 stick butter
½ cup chicken base
6 pounds potatoes, peeled
½ gallon water
1 quart half-and-half
Bacon bits, cheddar cheese, and scallions for garnishing

Preparation:

Combine celery, onions, butter, chicken base, and water in a large stockpot. Cook until potatoes are done. Using an immersion blender, blend, and add half-and-half slowly until soup coats the back of a spoon. Garnish with bacon bits, cheddar cheese, and scallions.

1782 Madison
901.272.1277

The Bar-B-Q Shop

One Of A Kind

I have been a fan of the Bar-B-Q Shop's creation, the Texas Toast Bar-B-Q Sandwich, from the early days, when they were "Brady and Lil's." They also are the creators of Bar-B-Q Spaghetti. Frank Vernon is now semi-retired, and his son Eric is doing a fabulous job. National press is all over the Bar-B-Q Shop. It was Voted #1 Bar-B-Q restaurant in America by the Food Network.

The Bar-B-Q Shop Seasoned Baked Chicken

Ingredients:

2 pounds chicken wings or chicken breasts
Salt, season to your satisfaction
Pepper, season to your satisfaction
1 large onion, sliced
2 cups cold water

Preparation:

Place all seasoned chicken in a pot. Cover with a sliced onion. Add water. Bake in a 325 degree oven until tender. Heavily sprinkle Dancing Pigs Dry Seasoning on your meat.

Central BBQ 2249 Central 901.272.9377

Go With a Winner

At Central, the meat is rubbed with a "secret combination" of dry spices. Their rapturous ribs are certainly no secret around Memphis. When it comes to ranking the top local Bar-B-Q restaurants, Central has been in the top three for over a decade. But why stop at Bar-B-Q? Central offers an impressive Portabella sandwich and the half-inch-thick Bar-B-Q Bologna sandwich is no slouch either.

Bologna Marinade

Ingredients:

2 medium onions, chopped
2 Tablespoons butter
1 Tablespoon thyme
1 Tablespoon ginger, minced or ground
1½ Tablespoons garlic, minced
2 Tablespoons cider vinegar
1½ pitcher domestic draft beer
2 Tablespoons brown sugar, packed
1 cup ketchup
Pinch salt
Pinch black pepper

Preparation:

Combine onion, spices, and butter in pot, and sauté at a low temp until caramelized. Then add liquid, boil off all alcohol, and add salt and pepper to taste.

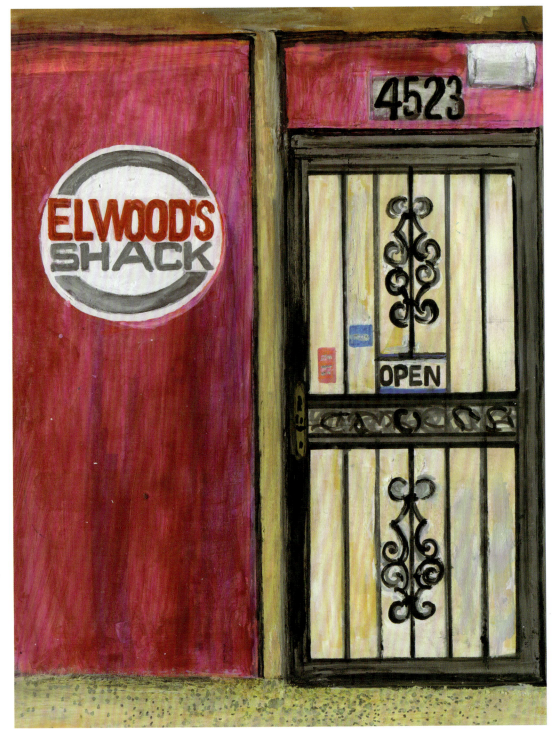

Elwood's Shack
4523 Summer
901.761.9898

Park It Right Here

This is a very casual restaurant that appears to be just an outcropping of a big-box store's parking lot. Don't be fooled. This "shack" has quite an alluring menu from breakfast to dinner—and brunch on weekends. Elwood's Shack is known for its Bar-B-Q: ribs, sandwich, or pizza; but brunch offers a creative Cheddar Quiche Baked in a Potato Nest and Eggs Sardou. Yes. Eggs Sardou in Memphis.

Spicy Maytag Blue Cheese and Jalapeño Cole Slaw

Ingredients:

- 1 medium head purple cabbage
- 5 large jalapeños, deseeded and sliced paper thin
- 1 Tablespoon sea salt
- 1 Tablespoon black pepper
- 1 teaspoon garlic powder
- 1 teaspoon onion powder
- ¼ cup red wine vinegar
- ¼ cup soy sauce
- ½ cup mayonnaise
- 2 Tablespoons Creole mustard
- 2 Tablespoons honey
- ¼ cup parmesan cheese
- 1 pound crumbled Maytag blue cheese

Preparation:

Quarter and remove core of purple cabbage. Slice each cabbage quarter against the grain with a knife, creating thin strips. Combine cabbage, jalapeños, and cheeses. Mix remaining dry and wet ingredients in a bowl, and mix with a whisk. Combine mixture with cabbage, and yum yum get you some!

1762 Lamar   901.272.1523    Payne's

Fill 'Er Up!

Forty three years ago Harold and Flora Payne converted this gas station into a Bar-B-Q restaurant like no other. There's a good reason the chopped pork sandwiches are the best sellers here! No seasonings are used during the entire day of cooking… very slow cooking over charcoal. Result? Terrifically tender and screamingly smoky! The restaurant remains in the Payne family today. And so does the secret sauce recipe.

Payne's Bar-B-Q Beans

Ingredients:

2½ cans pork and beans
½ cup brown sugar
2 Tablespoons onion powder
2 Tablespoons garlic powder
¼ cup Payne's mild BBQ sauce
¼ cup smoked shoulder, including fat and outside meat of shoulder

Preparation:

Place all ingredients in a slow cooker, and cook for 45–60 minutes.

A Dozen Dishes not to Miss

1. Cafe Keough–Walk into this architectural gem built in 1904, and relish the Brie and Fig Jam Croissant.
2. Cafe Society–Cafe Classic Seafood Bisque. Always amazing!
3. The Crazy Noodle–Korean Beef Noodle Soup and Vegetable Noodle Soup. Large in flavor, no need to waver.
4. Katie's Kitchen–Creamed Spinach Casserole—way up on the Totem Pole.
5. Evelyn & Olive–Fried Green Tomatoes cooked to perfection: lightly breaded served with Boom-Boom sauce. This spicy remoulade rocks!
6. Half Shell–Jumbo Fried Shrimp, Hand-Breaded and Deep Fried. A favorite of mine in lieu of wine… served with a very tasty tartar sauce!
7. Lunchbox Eats–Holiday Break Chicken is chicken salad made with a stellar secret creamy dressing on top of buttery cornbread.
8. Newbys–The Original Marinated Chicken Sandwich from 1975 is still very much alive! This is no dive! (Don't tell, but I scarfed my first MCS over 35 years ago!)
9. Pete & Sam's–Sausage Pizza with a thin crust and enough cheddar cheese to appease. Geez Louise!
10. Ronnie Grisanti's Italian Restaurant–Asparagus Bisque with Butter Poached Maine Lobster. Exceptional!
11. Slider Inn–Not to shun. Luscious indeed—this Lobster Roll takes the lead.
12. Tug's–A terrific Sirloin Hamburger—75% lean, 25% fat—served on a sweet sourdough bun.

Foodie Alert! Four Eateries on the Rise…

Belle Tavern… Modern bar with old-school speakeasy feel offers late night menu. Feeling macho? Try a Tavern Nacho. Entrance on Barboro Alley.

Raven & Lily… Owner/chef Justin Young puts a unique twist on a Cobb Salad. Let's just say the others are bygones. On Highway 64 in Oakland, TN (worth the drive).

Elwood's Shells… Tim Bednanski is serving succulent seafood: black drum, crawfish, shrimp, clams, oysters, po-boys, and jambalaya. Located behind Elwood's Shack at 4523 Summer.

Catherine and Mary's… Another Ticer/Hudman treasure in the Hotel Chisca building on Main. Outstanding is the Grilled Quail with Polenta, Pancetta, and Maitake Ragu… Wa-Hoo!

Keep the joy of loving God in your heart and share this joy with all you meet, especially your family.
—Mother Teresa of Calcutta

about Joy Bateman

An avowed foodie and talented artist, Joy Bateman is happy to blend these two passions to once again pay homage to the bustling restaurant scene in her beloved hometown of Memphis. *The Art of Dining® in Memphis 3* is the eighth book in the *Art of Dining®* series, and the third one about Memphis. Joy has worked as a senior account executive for *Memphis* magazine for the past 18 years and is active locally in the National Association of Women Business Owners (NAWBO Memphis), the Memphis Restaurant Association and Kiwanis Memphis.

Joy treasures spending time with her family, including husband Bill; three adult children Anna, Brown, and William; and four adorable grandchildren. Joy credits her parents, Joyce and Lester Gingold, with encouraging her creative pursuits. She is happiest when everyone, ages one to 95, can gather for a family meal. Breaking bread together is a blessing, whether at home or at one of Memphis' outstanding restaurants.

Obladee, oblada, life goes on . . .
—The Beatles